# Implementing the Automated Library System

by John Corbin

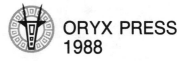

ORYX PRESS
1988

The rare Arabian Oryx is believed to have inspired the myth of the unicorn. This desert antelope became virtually extinct in the early 1960s. At that time several groups of international conservationists arranged to have 9 animals sent to the Phoenix Zoo to be the nucleus of a captive breeding herd. Today the Oryx population is nearly 800, and over 400 have been returned to reserves in the Middle East.

Copyright © 1988 by The Oryx Press
2214 North Central at Encanto
Phoenix, Arizona 85004-1483

Published simultaneously in Canada

Printed and Bound in the United States of America

∞ The paper used in this publication meets the minimum requirements of American National Standard for Information Science—Permanence of Paper for Printed Library Materials, ANSI Z39.48, 1984.

**Library of Congress Cataloging-in-Publication Data**

Corbin, John Boyd.
  Implementing the automated library system.

  Bibliography: p.
  Includes index.
  1. Libraries—Automation.  I. Title.
Z678.9.C633  1988   025.3'0285
ISBN 0-89774-455-1                          88-19650

# Contents

# List of Figures

# Preface

The purpose of this book is to provide a practical handbook and guide for integrating automation into existing library functions. As a companion volume to the author's *Managing the Library Automation Project* (Oryx Press, 1985), this book addresses the problems that will be encountered during the transition from manual to automated routines which occur after the hardware and software for a system have been acquired, installed, and tested. The emphasis is on the steps of the automation integration project, the impact of automation on existing functions, the changes that should and will take place, and the proper management of these changes.

*Implementing the Automated Library System* is intended for library managers who will be intimately involved in the exacting work of integrating automation into an existing library function. It will also be useful to senior library management staff who wish to learn more about the automated functions they indirectly manage and to staff who wish to understand better the automated function in which they work. While the emphasis is on implementing automated acquisitions, cataloging, and circulation functions, managers of other functions may also find the book useful, since the process will be essentially the same for their activities.

The text of the book is organized into 11 chapters. The first chapter provides an overview of automated library functions and the second chapter, an overview of the automation integration project. The remaining chapters describe the steps of the project, including organizational and management structure, tasks and procedures, job design and staffing, space planning and design, workstations, documentation, database conversion, computer operations, and automated function activation and evaluation.

The author wishes to acknowledge his gratitude to Dana Rooks, who read the manuscript and offered many useful suggestions for its improvement. Appreciation must also be expressed to my colleagues in the University of Houston Libraries and the School of Library and Information Sciences at the University of North Texas.

# Chapter 1
# Automated Library Functions

A library is composed of a number of sets of related activities called *functions*, of which acquiring, cataloging, organizing, and circulating informational materials; providing access to information; and providing personnel, fiscal, and building services are examples. These functions, which usually but not always conform to traditional organizational chart lines, are often grouped into public, technical, and administrative departments or divisions.

The purpose of this introductory chapter is to provide general background information and an overview of an automated library function, its component elements, and its structure. The chapter includes the following topics:

- Definition of an automated library function
- Elements of an automated library function
- Structure of an automated library function
- Impacts of automation on a function

## DEFINITION OF AN AUTOMATED LIBRARY FUNCTION

When a computer is used to support a library function—that is, when a computer performs some of the basic processing operations in a function such as acquiring, cataloging, and circulating materials; or providing access to information—a computer-based or *automated library function* results.

In an automated library function, staff and computer share responsibility for performing work. For example, a staff member might perform the first five processing operations; the computer, the next 25 operations; the staff member, the next three operations; and so on. Due to this sharing of responsibilities, today's automated library functions actually should be referred to as "human-machine systems," or literally "functions in which humans are assisted by a computer." The computer is merely a tool, albeit a marvelous one, enabling librarians to do something more rapidly, more accurately, or less expensively than by manual methods. Completely automatic or automated library functions, in which no human intervention and control are necessary, do not exist and are not likely to exist until the end of the century or beyond.

## ELEMENTS OF AN AUTOMATED LIBRARY FUNCTION

An automated library function has a number of elements, regardless of its nature or complexity, the type of library in which it operates (academic, public, special, or school), or the type of service it performs (technical, public, or administrative). A block diagram depicting these elements is shown in Figure 1-1.

**FIGURE 1-1. A Block Diagram Depicting the Elements of an Automated Library Function**

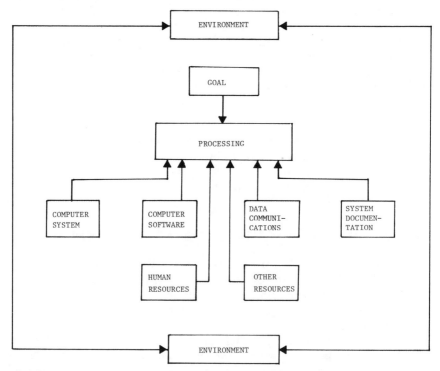

### A Goal

A primary element of an automated library function is its goal, the purpose or reason why the set of activities comprising the function was organized. This goal will be the focal point for integrating automation into the function and for operating and managing the activities after automation of the function is complete. The goal of an automated library function is discussed further in Chapter 3.

## Processing

A second element of an automated library function is processing, which consists of sets of step-by-step operations performed in an orderly and predetermined sequence on information, materials, or other items to achieve a desired end result, such as a service or a product. The information, materials, or other items are processed as the step-by-step operations are completed. Processing in an automated library function is discussed further in Chapter 4.

## The Computer System

A third element of an automated library function is the computer system supporting the function's activities. The supporting computer may be a microcomputer, a minicomputer, or a mainframe. The size needed will depend upon the nature of the function being automated, the number of functions to be supported by the computer, the volume of processing activity anticipated, the size of the information files that must be retained in machine storage, and the funds available to the library.

One concern of the manager of the automated function should be whether or not the computer system can provide the function with adequate support. That is, the computer must provide sufficient computing power and capabilities to enable the automated function to be operated effectively and efficiently. First, the computer must have sufficient internal memory to store the operating system and application software in use at the moment, process the volume of work required by the automated function, and enable sufficient users to be online to it at the same time, with a capacity for future growth. Second, the computer system must have sufficient auxiliary storage for all the files essential to the automated function, with a capacity for future growth. Third, the computer must be able to accommodate the number of terminals and other peripheral equipment needed to support the automated function, with capacity to grow in the future. Fourth, sufficient terminals and other devices, such as scanners and printers, must actually be available to enable the function to achieve its objectives. Another concern of the manager of the automated function should be whether or not the computer system can provide the function with consistent computing capabilities—that is, whether the system will be operating properly and available for use by the automated function as close to 100% of the expected availability time as possible.

A primary advantage to locating the computer in the library is that the library can retain management control over the system and not be dependent upon another department or agency to operate and maintain its computer system or supply it with computing power. The disadvantage to having the computer in the library is that special air-conditioned and humidity-controlled quarters might have to be provided for the system. In addition, the library will have to train its staff to operate and manage the system or hire additional staff for these responsibilities.

The advantages to having the computer supporting an automated function in another department or agency serving the library is that the library would not have to provide either space and a controlled environment for housing the system or the staff required for its operation, management, and maintenance. The major disadvantage is that the library might not be able to control the hours the computer is available for its use. Staff in the computing center may not be available at the right times to start, stop, operate, and maintain the computer system. Also, if the computer supporting its automated function is shared with other departments or agencies, the library may have problems gaining sufficient auxiliary storage, assistance in enhancing its software, and priority on machine use. Computer operations are discussed further in Chapter 10.

## Computer Software

A fourth element of an automated library function is the software supporting its activities. The automated function cannot operate without computer software, which are the sets of step-by-step instructions that command the machine to perform its share of the processing. The software may have been developed by a commercial vendor or another library or organization, or it may have been developed locally from scratch. It may be maintained for the library by the vendor, by another library or organization, by library staff, or by a computing center serving the library. The library may be the sole user of the software or it may be shared with other libraries located nearby or at a distance.

Regardless of its origin or maintenance or who uses it, the software supporting an automated library function can be characterized as being either stand-alone or integrated. Stand-alone software supports only one automated function, such as acquisitions, circulation, cataloging, or serials control. The software operates in isolation from all other software the library might use; information in its online files is not shared with any other automated function. Stand-alone software is neither economical nor efficient for the library in the long run, although it may be sufficient on a short-term basis. For automation of the library to be realistic and economical, it must be organized to support the flow and use of information both within and between the various functions comprising the library organization. Most library functions need to freely share bibliographic, textual, transaction, and management information among themselves.

It may be more desirable that the software supporting an automated library function be part of an integrated set supporting several other functions. An integrated library system is a set of software for functions such as acquisitions, cataloging, circulation, and serials control, which are interrelated and interacting and which share common information and files. An integrated system will be more economical and efficient for a library than stand-alone software in the long run, because information can be created once, then stored in files to be accessed by any automated function within the library needing it.

Most integrated computer software supporting library functions is designed, prepared, and supplied by the same organization or vendor, although success is now being achieved with interfacing the software of one vendor with that of other vendors. For example, the software for an automated acquisitions function of one vendor can be interfaced with the software of an automated circulation function of a different vendor. These two sets of software may in turn be interfaced with the online catalog software of a third vendor. Electronic links between the functions must enable them to share information in their respective files, or else integration of the modules will not be possible. The advantage to this approach is that the best software available on the market for a particular function can be acquired by a library, on the assumption that one vendor alone cannot provide software of a uniform quality to support all the various components of an integrated system. However, problems in making the functions work together can easily arise, especially in exchanging information effectively and efficiently between the interfaced sets of software. When such problems do arise, there may be a tendency of the vendors of the separate modules to lay the blame on the other vendors.

## Data Communications

A fifth element of an automated library function is data communications. Through data communications, commands and information can flow from the computer system supporting the automated function to the points in the library where processing is required, even though the machine may be located in another part of the building or in another building blocks or miles from the library.

The data communications channels could be direct-connect cables, leased telephone line connections, dial-up telephone line connections, or local area network connections. A discussion of each of these can be found in Chapter 6.

## System Documentation

Documentation, in the form of memoranda, reports, and manuals, is a sixth element essential to an automated library function. Documentation refers to the written descriptions of various aspects of the automated function to be used by library staff and others for training, reference, and quality control purposes while operating, managing, and maintaining the function. Documentation for an automated library function is discussed further in Chapter 8.

## Human Resources

A seventh element of an automated library function is the human resources needed to share processing with the computer supporting the function; provide management and leadership for the function; and operate, manage, and maintain the computer system supporting the function.

People are needed on a day-to-day basis in an automated library function to share the performance of processing operations with the computer supporting the activities of the function. Staff must initiate processes, provide the computer with information to be processed, and make decisions during processing steps and regarding the services to be provided or the products to be produced. Those activities not supported by the computer system also must be performed by people.

Also, people are needed to manage the automated library function and to provide leadership to its staff. Managers on several levels must plan and organize the work to be done; recruit, hire, train, evaluate, and supervise the staff who will perform the day-to-day operations; coordinate the activities of the function with those of other functions in the library; prepare budget requests for the function's activities; and provide leadership and inspiration to its staff.

In addition, people are needed to operate, manage, and maintain the computer system supporting the automated library function. Staff members must start up, monitor, and shut down the computer and online systems when necessary; initiate and monitor batch processes; and operate and maintain the computer's peripheral equipment, while being themselves supervised in these activities by other staff. Still others must provide corrective and preventive maintenance for both hardware and software supporting the automated library function. Those people who operate and manage the computer system may be on the library's staff or on the staff of a computing center serving the library. Corrective and preventive maintenance of hardware and software typically is provided by a vendor. Staffing an automated library function is discussed further in Chapter 5.

## Other Resources

Other resources, such as information, equipment and furniture, consumable supplies, and monetary resources, are an eighth element of an automated library function.

Information can be viewed as a non-consumable resource utilized by an automated function as it is operated. Information stored in resource files is utilized over and over again as other information is processed by the computer. For example, information in borrower, vendor, and bibliographic files is accessed repeatedly, but is neither consumed nor depreciated as the function operates.

Equipment such as computer terminals, printers, modems, telephones, typewriters, calculators, and the like will be required by the staff as they perform their day-to-day activities of operating and managing the automated library function. Desks, tables, chairs, cabinets, shelving, printer stands, acoustic covers for printers, filing cabinets, a conference table, and other furniture will also be necessary.

Supplies are consumed as an automated library function is operated. Paper, custom forms, labels, printer ribbons, magnetic tapes, cleaning materials, and electrical energy, in addition to pencils, pens, paperclips, rubber bands, and other common office supplies, are necessary to the automated function.

Monetary resources are needed to acquire the physical and human resources necessary to operate and maintain an automated library function. Since an automated function must operate within the limits of a budget imposed upon it, the availability of funds dictates the amount of other resources available for its operations and, therefore, the type, quality, and quantity of its output.

## Environment

A ninth and last element of an automated library function is environment. The automated function must exist and be operated in an environment designed for its needs; it must have sufficient physical space to perform efficiently and be provided with proper levels of lighting, temperature, humidity, noise control, and cleanliness. Color and graphics can further enhance the working environment for both staff and library users. The environment for an automated library function is discussed further in Chapter 6.

## STRUCTURE OF AN AUTOMATED LIBRARY FUNCTION

To the uninitiated, a library function may seem so complex that the task of automating it appears beyond comprehension. Even a good starting point might appear totally elusive. The systems approach provides such a beginning. Using the systems approach, the librarian has a tool or method for separating a complex library function into a number of smaller and thus more manageable parts that can be more readily studied and understood as automation is introduced.

## The Systems Approach

A *system* is defined as a set of independent yet interrelated and interacting parts organized to achieve a desired end result or goal. Viewing a function in this manner is called *the systems approach.*

Systems have several characteristics of interest to the librarian attempting to automate a library function. One of the most important of these characteristics is that every system can be separated into two or more smaller systems. The result of this division is another level of systems. Each system on this second level can in turn be divided still further into even smaller systems on a third level. The process of separating a system into smaller and smaller component systems can continue as far as is possible or practical.

Another characteristic of a system is that the systems on all levels of its hierarchical structure are self-contained and independent of each other. However, while each system is independent of all others, none can exist by itself. Each system is an integral part of the larger system.

## An Automated Library Function as a System

Library functions such as acquiring, cataloging, and circulating informational materials; providing access to information; and providing personnel, fiscal, and building services can be viewed as systems. As a matter of fact, automated library functions frequently are referred to as automated library systems.

The automated library function can be viewed as an independent and self-contained system, interacting and interrelated with other functions in the library. The function will either share information or rely upon other functions within the library to generate or provide information required for its operation. For example, in some technical library functions, materials and information are partially processed in one function, then passed on to other functions for completion of the work.

Using the systems approach, a library function can be separated into a number of smaller component functions. Three levels seem sufficient for most automated library functions. A general model of these levels is shown in Figure 1-2. The function as a whole is Level 1.

The component functions on Level 2 of the hierarchy, which are broad or general in nature, are referred to as *activities* in this book. All work within a function must be accounted for in one or another of its

**FIGURE 1-2. A General Model of the Levels of an Automated Library Function**

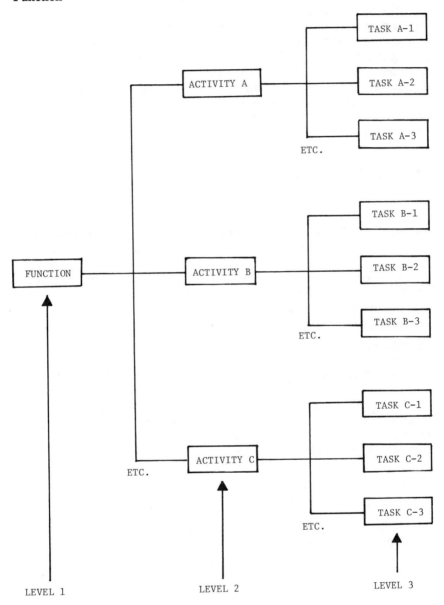

component activities on Level 2. Each activity is independent of, but also interrelated and interacting with, all other activities on that level. Activities are discussed further in Chapter 3.

Each activity on Level 2 can be separated still further into two or more smaller component functions, referred to in this book as *tasks* on Level 3 of the hierarchy. All work within an activity must be accounted for in one or another of its component tasks. Each task is independent of, but also interrelated and interacting with, all other tasks on that level. The step-by-step procedures comprising the work of a function are performed at this lowest level in the hierarchy. Tasks are discussed further in Chapter 4.

## IMPACTS OF AUTOMATION ON A FUNCTION

Automating a library function will require considerable change in existing activities if the full potential benefits of computer use are to be realized. The changes will transform the nonautomated function into an entirely new, more effective and efficient function better able to serve its users.

Many changes should or will take place in a function as it is automated. Few aspects of an existing function will remain unaffected after automated activities are successfully integrated into it.

### Operations

A major impact of automation on an existing function will be in its operations. Operations in an automated function will be different, more complex, and will require more precision in their execution than in a function with no automation. Automated operations require smooth interaction to avoid errors and delays in service and are more sensitive to dysfunction than their traditional manual counterparts. Errors made in the workflow of the automated function, or steps omitted, create a ripple effect in its operation. Usually, operations cannot be omitted or rearranged without serious repercussions in an automated function, and when one operation fails, the workflow could stop or the system could fail completely. This is not always the case in a function operated manually.

### Staffing

Automation of an existing function will have a major impact on staffing. The use of automation could result in a reduction of staff necessary in a function, although some staff who are eliminated could be retained and shifted to other programs or functions. More often, automation requires a major restructuring of jobs and a subsequent reassignment of duties for all staff in the system. No level of staff in the function will be unaffected by automation. All staff will have to be re-oriented and retrained to operate within the automated function.

## Access to Files

An exciting impact of automation could be a decentralization of files supporting a function. Once a function is automated and its files are under computer control, access to records previously available only in one location can now be made accessible to many in a decentralized manner. For example, the shelf list, which previously was available only to staff who came to technical services, now can be available to any staff or user with access to a computer terminal. The same is true for the traditional card catalog when an online catalog is implemented.

This decentralization of access to files can have a tremendous impact on how the public perceives and uses the library. It also will assist in breaking down departmental barriers and could foster new interdepartmental relationships.

## Organizational and Management Structure

One change that might take place when automation is successfully integrated into a library function is in the organizational and management structure of the function. Lines between the new, automated function and others in the library could blur and shift, and relationships and interfaces between it and other functions could be altered. A totally new and better organizational structure could evolve as a result of automation.

## Services

An important and beneficial impact of library automation can be seen in improved services to users, because the computer is capable of performing repetitive and routine work faster and more accurately than can humans. In addition, since an increased amount of work can be performed in an automated library function, the computer could enable the library to offer new services never before possible with a manual system.

## Costs

Aside from the problem of job displacement, the cost of operating an automated library function is its most controversial aspect. A prevalent rule of thumb for library automation has been that unless an automated function can provide the same services for less cost, or better services for the same cost, the effort should not be undertaken. But it must be remembered that an automated function often is radically different from a manual one, so it is difficult to obtain accurate cost figures for a comparison between manual and automated activities. Implementation of an automated library function is expensive, and the costs of maintaining it could be more expensive than the manual function it replaces.

## ADDITIONAL READINGS

Ackoff, R.L. "Towards a System of Systems Concepts." *Management Science* 17 (July 1971): 661-71.

Adelson, Marvin. "The Systems Approach: A Perspective." *Wilson Library Bulletin* 42 (March 1968): 711-15.

Athey, Thomas H. "Fundamental Systems Concepts." *Journal of Systems Management* 28 (November 1977): 42-45.

Bellomy, F.L. "The Systems Approach Solves Library Problems." *ALA Bulletin* 62 (October 1968): 1121-25.

Bertalanffy, Ludwig von. *General Systems Theory: Foundations, Development, Applications.* New York: Braziller, 1968.

Churchman, C. West. *The Systems Approach.* Rev. and Updated Ed. New York: Dell, 1983.

Corbin, John. "The Automated Library System." In *Managing the Library Automation Project.* Phoenix: Oryx Press, 1985: 3-16.

Emery, Frederick E. *Systems Thinking: Selected Readings.* Harmondsworth, England: Penguin Books, 1969.

Kast, Fremont E., and James E. Rosenzweig. "General Systems Theory: Applications for Organization and Management." In *Strategies for Library Administration: Concepts and Approaches*, by Charles R. McClure and Alan R. Samuels. Littleton, CO: Libraries Unlimited, 1982: 359-77.

Katz, Daniel and Robert L. Kahn. "Organizations and the System Concept." In *Reader in Library and Information Services*, edited by Michael M. Reynolds and Evelyn H. Daniel. New York: Microcard Editions, 1974: 7-23.

Kemeny, John G. *Man and the Computer.* New York: Scribner, 1972.

Kilgour, Frederick G. "Systems Concepts and Libraries." *College & Research Libraries* 28 (May 1967): 167-70.

Mansfield, Una. "The Systems Movement: An Overview for Information Scientists." *Journal of the American Society for Information Science* 33 (November 1982): 375-82.

Mattessich, Richard. "Systems Approach: Its Variety of Aspects." *Journal of the American Society for Information Science* 33 (November 1982): 383-94.

Nadler, Gerald. "Concept of Systems." In *Work Design: A Systems Concept.* Rev. ed. New York: Irwin, 1970: 21-47.

# Chapter 2
# The Automation Integration Project

Once an automated system has been acquired by a library and its hardware and software have been installed and tested, the system must be implemented. That is, the new activities must be integrated into an existing library function.

There is no right or wrong approach to integrating automation into a library function. Different people can achieve the same results by using different means. Approaching the integration process as a project enables the effort to be properly planned. The purpose of this chapter is to suggest a methodology for establishing and controlling such a project. The chapter includes the following topics:

- The integration process
- Project goals and constraints
- Project activities
- Staff for the project
- The project budget
- Project progress

## THE INTEGRATION PROCESS

Integrating automation into a library function is a blending of two systems—the new and the existing—into one (Figure 2-1), whereby attributes of the new are substituted for those of the existing function. The result will be an automated function with a new set of attributes. The process will not be rapid, nor will it be easy, and will require resolve on the part of all staff, a planned approach to the transition, and, in some cases, the firm backing of the library's top management.

Planning will have a critical impact on the successful integration of automation into a function. Good planning will enable the librarian to control the process, increase the chances that the automated operations will be installed with minimum problems, and ensure effective results.

## FIGURE 2-1. The Integration of Automation into an Existing Library Function

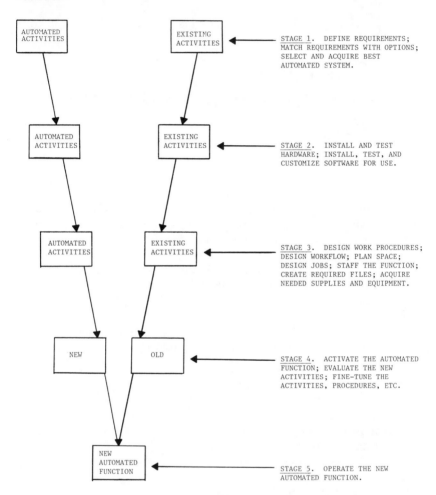

Inadequate and ineffective planning could delay the integration process, waste financial resources, reduce acceptance of the automated function by staff and users, and possibly do long-term damage to the organization through the generation of ill will and loss of credibility. Merely introducing computer-based activities into an existing library function without sound planning and follow-through will not automatically improve the function.

## PROJECT GOALS AND CONSTRAINTS

As a first step to organizing the automation integration project, goals and constraints should be established.

### Project Goals

Project goals will provide guidelines to follow when integrating automation into a library function.

*Example*: The goals of the project are to develop an automated function that: (1) is responsive to the needs of its users; (2) is streamlined; (3) can process all materials within two weeks with no backlogs; (4) can identify the location of any item in process in the function; (5) makes all online files available to anyone in the library with access to a terminal; (6) eliminates the need for all paper files; and (7) produces the maximum output at a minimum cost while retaining the highest possible quality.

Goals should be documented, discussed, and accepted by the staff of the function and by other appropriate people before the integration project is begun.

### Project Constraints

Any constraints to be placed on the integration project by library management or others should be identified. These constraints will limit or place conditions on the undertaking.

*Example*: Constraints on the project are that: (1) existing staff must be utilized in the automated function, with attrition or transfers being the only means of eliminating positions; (2) only five computer terminals will be available to the function for five years; (3) the space for the automated function must be reduced by 25% from the existing space; and (4) the cost of implementing the automated function must not exceed $——.

Constraints should also be documented, discussed, and approved before work is begun. The project goals and constraints can be discussed and approved at the same time.

## PROJECT ACTIVITIES

A strategy or plan for completing the automation integration project should be developed to guide the efforts of the team responsible for its completion. In preparing the strategy, the librarian might identify the activities of the project, then schedule the activities.

The work to be done in the project should be separated into a number of activities that must be completed. Each activity can contain a number of smaller activities or steps. The exact number of events in the project will depend upon the nature and complexity of the function being automated.

The typical activities of an automation integration project shown in Figures 2-2 and 2-3 give an overview of the process. Not all activities can be completed simultaneously, because some steps involve different and more difficult and time-consuming tasks than others. In many cases, one or several steps must be completed before others can be begun. The plan should be dynamic; activities should be altered as work on the project progresses and as new conditions and situations arise.

**FIGURE 2-2. A Gantt Chart for an Automation Integration Project**

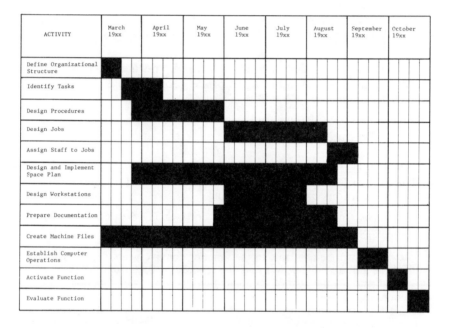

After the activities of the project have been developed, discussed, and accepted, a schedule or calendar for completing them should be prepared. The activities to be completed, their beginning and ending times, and the duration of time expected to complete each can be shown in either a Gantt chart or a network chart. The relationships between the activities can easily be inferred from studying either chart. The Gantt chart is easier to construct and revise than the network chart, but relationships between activities are easier to visualize using the network chart.

A sample Gantt chart for an automation integration project is shown in Figure 2-2 and an alternative network chart for the same project is shown in Figure 2-3.

**FIGURE 2-3. An Alternative Network Chart for an Automation Integration Project**

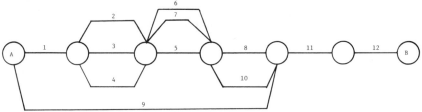

A=Begin Activities

B=End Activities

1–Define organizational structure
2–Identify tasks
3–Design procedures
4–Design jobs
5–Assign staff to jobs
6–Design and implement space plan
7–Design workstations
8–Prepare documentation
9–Create machine files
10–Establish computer operations
11–Activate function
12–Evaluate function

## STAFF FOR THE PROJECT

A number of people must be organized to successfully complete the activities identified for the automation integration project.

### The Project Manager

A project manager should be assigned responsibility for the successful completion of the integration project. More than likely, this person will be the chief executive officer designate of the function to be automated. If not, project management can be delegated to another person on the staff of the function to be automated.

The specific functions or responsibilities of the project manager will depend upon his or her experience and capabilities and the nature of the undertaking. The project manager might:

1. Establish goals and objectives for the project in conjunction with other staff of the function to be automated, with library users, and with other interested people.
2. Analyze the project to identify the activities that must be completed in order to integrate automation into the function properly.
3. Select, organize, direct, and coordinate a project team that will be responsible for completing the individual activities of the project.

4. Establish and maintain communication and a good working relationship with the library's systems or automation librarian, the supplier of the hardware and software that will support the automated function, and others who will be contributing to the successful implementation of the new system.
5. Keep the library director and others informed about the project's progress and problems.

## The Project Team

A team can be assembled to assist the project manager in completing the project successfully. This not only provides the project manager with needed assistance during the activities of the project, but involves the staff in the process as well. The team can be composed of key staff, such as unit managers of the function being automated.

The specific functions or responsibilities assigned to the team will depend upon the size of the staff and the nature of the function to be automated. The team might:

1. Assist the project manager in planning the project.
2. Manage the specific activities identified for the project, perhaps by assigning each person a specific activity to oversee.
3. Provide the project manager with ideas and advice pertaining to the various activities of the project.
4. Provide general support for the project and for the automated function.

## Other Project Resource People

A number of other people will be resources to the automation integration project, including the library's automation librarian, the staff of the function being automated, vendor representatives, staff of other automated functions, and miscellaneous people.

The library's systems or automation librarian will be an invaluable resource to those integrating automation into a library function. The automation librarian should have detailed knowledge of both hardware and software supporting the automated function and of automated systems in general, as well as general insights into implementing automated systems that can be shared with the project team, and an intimacy with the library's master plan for automation and ways individual functions fit into that plan. This person also can provide assistance in coordinating or interfacing the procedures to be developed for the automated function with those of other manual and automated functions within the library to ensure their compatibility.

While the project team might provide most of the guidance for integrating automation into a library function, the advice of other staff of the function being automated certainly should be solicited as often as possible. These people can provide valuable information about the existing function and about the needs and demands on a new one. Their continued involvement in the project can facilitate their support and approval of the evolving automated function.

Representatives of the vendor who sold to the library the hardware and software supporting the automated system being implemented can provide valuable assistance to the project staff. These people can supply verbal and written information about the system, guidance in installing various aspects of the automated function, and orientation and training in its use.

The staff of other libraries having the same or a similar automated function can be helpful by demonstrating their systems, sharing experiences encountered during their automation projects, and providing encouragement to the library just beginning to develop its own automated function. Advice on integrating automation into a function and on potential problems that might be encountered or situations to be avoided can be helpful to a library not yet experienced with automated systems or with a particular vendor.

Many other people might be utilized, however briefly, during an automation project. These people could include purchasing agents, communications experts, carpenters, electronics engineers and technicians, air conditioning and heating experts, painters, hardware and software installers and maintenance staff, trainers for teaching the staff to operate and manage the automated function, and many others. Each will play a vital role in completion of the project.

## THE PROJECT BUDGET

An estimate of the funds needed to successfully integrate automation into an existing function should be prepared and submitted to the appropriate budget authorities for approval before the project is begun. The budget should include those expenses necessary to design and implement a new floor layout, purchase and install new workstations and other equipment and furniture, create any essential online databases, and acquire essential supplies to start using the automated system, plus any other expenses considered necessary to implement the new system. In many cases, the need for funds cannot be ascertained until after an integration activity has been started. In this case, the request for funds must be submitted at that time.

## PROJECT PROGRESS

Progress reports on the automation integration project should be made regularly to the library director, the staff of the function being automated, other staff in the library, and other interested persons. The reports might include verbal reports, written reports, and updated project calendars.

### Verbal Reports

Verbal progress reports can be made in formal or informal meetings of staff, governing and funding authorities, and others. The reports should include descriptions of work completed to date compared with estimated completion times, and any unexpected problems encountered since the last report.

### Written Reports

Written progress reports can be prepared for inclusion in a library-wide or departmental newsletter. Like verbal reports, written reports should include descriptions of work completed to date compared with estimated completion times, and any unexpected problems encountered since the last report.

### Updated Project Calendars

Still another means of keeping others informed about the project is to periodically update and distribute copies of the Gantt or network chart, whichever is used, outlining the activities of the project. If desired, the updated calendar can also be distributed during verbal reports and/or attached to any written reports that are distributed.

## ADDITIONAL READINGS

Brophy, P. "Managing the System Implementation Process." In *The Management of Polytechnic Libraries*. Gower Press, 1985: 84-103.

Burke, Jane. "Automation Planning and Implementation: Library and Vendor Responsibilities." In *Clinic on Library Applications of Data Processing (22nd: 1985: University of Illinois at Urbana-Champaign)*. Urbana: University of Illinois Graduate School of Library and Information Science, 1986: 46-58.

Cheatham, David. "The Systems Development Life Cycle as a Planning Methodology for Library Automation." *Information Technology in Libraries* 4 (September 1985): 208-14.

Cleland, David I. and William R. King, eds. *Project Management Handbook.* New York: Van Nostrand, 1983.

Cleland, David I. and William R. King. *System Analysis and Project Management.* 3rd ed. New York: McGraw-Hill, 1983.

Corbin, John. "Project Planning and Control." In *Managing the Library Automation Project.* Phoenix: Oryx Press, 1985: 56-71.

Lowry, Charles B. "Technology in Libraries: Six Rules for Management." *Library Hi Tech* 3 (1985): 27-9.

Luquire, Wilson. "Attitudes Toward Automation/Innovation in Academic Libraries." *Journal of Academic Librarianship* 8 (January 1983): 344-51.

Veaner, Allen B. "Major Decision Points in Library Automation." *College & Research Libraries* 31 (September 1970): 299-312.

Warheit, I.A. "The Automation of Libraries: Some Economic Considerations." *Special Libraries* 63 (January 1972): 1-7.

# Chapter 3
# Organizational and
# Management Structure

Good organizational and management structures are critical for a successful automated library function such as acquiring, cataloging, or circulating informational materials. The benefits of developing a sound organizational structure include a focusing on goals, an effective framework for the work to be performed, and an effective basis for management of a function. Once the work within an automated function has been organized, efforts must be made to ensure that the components are operated to achieve the goals of the function and that the units are coordinated with each other effectively and efficiently.

As automation is introduced into an existing function within the library, the opportunity should be taken to resolve any long-standing problems with its organizational and management structures that might exist. A certain amount of experimentation and risk-taking is desirable and often necessary to implement a highly effective and efficient automated function. Certainly, few if any of the benefits of automation can ever be realized if the existing function remains essentially unchanged after it is automated.

If an automated function is to achieve a higher level of performance and excellence than the one it replaced, it does not need "to do things of the same and better," but to do things in a completely different way and from a different perspective. For this reason, the function should be reviewed as if it were being organized for the first time. Even if the existing organizational structure is found to be the most effective for the automated environment, the review process can be beneficial by affirming this fact.

The purpose of this chapter is to discuss the development of appropriate organizational and management structures for an automated library function. Its topics include:

- Goals for the automated function
- Activities of the function
- Organizational and management units

- Management positions
- The chain of command
- The administrative group
- Communications channels
- Committees and projects
- The informal organization
- Flexibility

## GOALS FOR THE AUTOMATED FUNCTION

The first step to organizing an automated library function might be to establish its goals; these will consist of a primary purpose or mission for the function as a whole, and several secondary goals derived from the primary one. These goals will be the focal point for developing the organizational and management structures of the function and will serve as a guiding philosophy for its staff. The goals also will lend a sense of unity and direction to those who later will be learning to operate, use, and manage the function.

Of concern should be the primary goal of the automated function, the secondary goals of the function, and the compatibility of the goals.

### The Primary Goal of the Automated Function

The primary purpose or goal of the automated library function as a whole first should be defined. This statement will indicate what the function will be doing, such as acquiring materials or goods, producing a product, or providing a service. The goal should be general, open-ended, not prone to drastic change over time, and not readily measurable. It also should be clear and unambiguous.

*Example:* The primary goal of the automated acquisitions function is to acquire materials, through purchases, gifts, and exchanges, for addition to the library's collections.

*Example:* The primary goal of the automated cataloging function is to provide bibliographic access to materials in the library's collection and to process materials for use.

*Example:* The primary goal of the automated circulation function is to loan materials to borrowers in good standing and to ensure their timely return.

An automated library function will have the same primary goal as that of its parallel manual function. Using a computer does not alter the purpose of a function, but merely enables the library staff to perform its work faster, less expensively, and more accurately than a staff using manual methods.

## Secondary Goals of the Function

The primary goal of the automated library function should be separated into a number of smaller component or secondary goals. These secondary goals indicate how the overall goal of the function will be achieved. Secondary goals also should be general, open-ended, not prone to drastic changes over time, and not readily measurable, in addition to being clear and unambiguous.

> *Example*: The secondary goals of the automated acquisitions function are to: (1) provide for the rapid verification and searching of requests for acquisition; (2) order informational materials as rapidly as possible; (3) maintain accurate accounting records of orders and expenditures; (4) receive the ordered informational materials in an effective and efficient manner; (5) claim and cancel ordered informational materials when necessary; (6) enable appropriate inquiries into the function's database; and (7) enable the function's database to be easily maintained.

> *Example*: The secondary goals of the automated cataloging function are to: (1) provide effective and efficient bibliographic control and access to all informational materials in the library's collection in a manner consistent with national standards; (2) maintain an effective inventory of all materials for accountability purposes; (3) maintain the bibliographic and inventory database effectively and efficiently; and (4) rapidly mark and label informational materials for use.

> *Example*: The secondary goals of the automated circulation function are to: (1) provide for the rapid and accurate charging, discharging, and renewal of materials to users; (2) provide an effective means of placing holds on materials; (3) provide an effective means of handling recalls of materials; (4) provide for the effective management of circulation fines and fees; (5) produce overdue notices in a timely manner; (6) enable appropriate inquiries into the function's database; and (7) enable the function's database to be easily maintained.

The secondary goals of an automated function, derived from its primary goal, will form the basis of its activities, discussed below.

Sources of information for identifying the secondary goals of an automated function can be the librarian's professional knowledge and experience as to what will be required to accomplish the primary goal of the function, and the creativity and imagination of the librarian.

## Compatibility of the Goals

The proposed goals of the automated library function should be compared with others in the goals structure of the library to verify that there are no conflicts. If the automated function's proposed goals are inconsistent or in conflict with others in the library, then this problem must be resolved before development of the automated function continues.

There should be an unbroken chain of goals leading from the mission of the library as a whole down to that of the automated function. To illustrate this, a typical library goals structure is shown in Figure 3-1. The mission of the library and several broad philosophical goals derived from the mission are shown. Goals at the top of the hierarchy are the broadest, while those on the lowest level where the automated function will exist are the most specific. Each goal must support, and not be in conflict with, the goals above it or on its same level.

**FIGURE 3-1. A Typical Goals Structure of a Library**

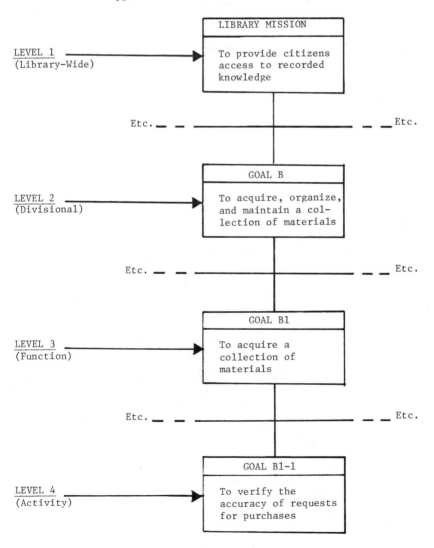

## ACTIVITIES OF THE FUNCTION

The activities required to achieve the goals established for an automated library function should be identified. The activities of the automated function are derived from its goals.

An *activity* is defined as a major area of work considered necessary to achieve a specified goal of a function. All work within the automated function must be accounted for in one or another of its activities. The computer software supporting the automated function usually will be organized around activities. To illustrate the separation of an automated function into its component activities, Figure 3-2 shows the activities typical of automated acquisitions, cataloging, and circulation functions.

**FIGURE 3-2. Activities Typical of Automated Acquisitions, Cataloging, and Circulation Functions**

| AUTOMATED ACQUISITIONS FUNCTION | AUTOMATED CATALOGING FUNCTION | AUTOMATED CIRCULATION FUNCTION |
|---|---|---|
| Order Entry | Edit Cataloging | Charge |
| Order Verification and Checking | Original Cataloging | Discharge |
| Order Preparation | Marking and Labelling | Renewals |
| Order Receipt | Database Maintenance | Holds |
| Claiming and Cancelling | | Recalls |
| Fund Accounting | | Fines and Fees |
| | | Overdues and Other Notices |
| | | Database Maintenance |

## ORGANIZATIONAL AND MANAGEMENT UNITS

The activities comprising the automated library system must be grouped together into units. Each group of activities will become a unit of the organizational structure of the function, each with its own manager in charge.

Several factors should be studied before the activities of an automated function are grouped into organizational units. In some cases, one activity will form the basis of a single organizational unit, while in other cases, two or more activities can be grouped into the same organizational unit. The organizational groups required for an automated function will depend upon such factors as the number of staff to be assigned to each activity, the complexity of work within the activities, the similarity of the activities to each other, and the physical proximity of the activities to each other.

The librarian may wish to postpone grouping activities into organizational units until after, or at least simultaneous with, the identification of tasks, the design of procedures for each activity, and the design of jobs for the activities. These processes are described in

Chapter 4. Figure 3-3 illustrates an automated acquisitions function with two organizational units for six activities. Figure 3-4 illustrates an automated cataloging function with four units for four activities. Figure 3-5 illustrates an automated circulation function with three units for eight activities.

**FIGURE 3-3. An Automated Acquisitions Function with Two Organizational Units for Six Activities**

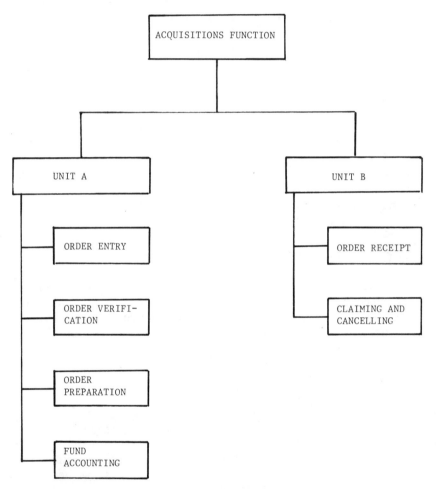

## The Number of Staff Assigned to Each Activity

The number of staff assigned to each activity might dictate how many activities can be grouped into one organizational unit of the

**FIGURE 3-4. An Automated Cataloging Function with Four Organizational Units for Four Activities**

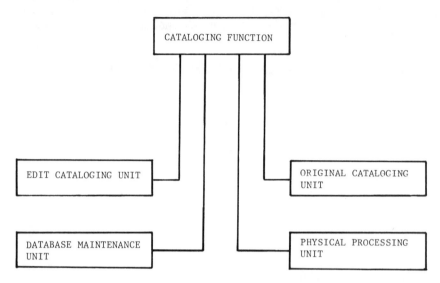

automated function. A manager usually is limited to directly supervising no more than five to eight staff.

## The Complexity of the Work within the Activities

The complexity of activities might dictate how many of them can be grouped together into one organizational unit. Complex activities require closer management. Therefore, the more complex the activities are, the fewer of them that can be grouped together for effective management.

## The Similarity of the Activities to Each Other

The similarity of activities to each other might dictate how many can be grouped together. Several similar activities might be grouped together to be managed by one person, while dissimilar activities might best be placed into separate organizational units under separate managers. If activities are dissimilar, the number grouped together should be small, because the manager placed in charge of the unit would require more knowledge of a variety of jobs. The more diverse the activities, the fewer that should be placed in the same grouping to be managed by one person.

**FIGURE 3-5. An Automated Circulation Function with Three Organizational Units for Eight Activities**

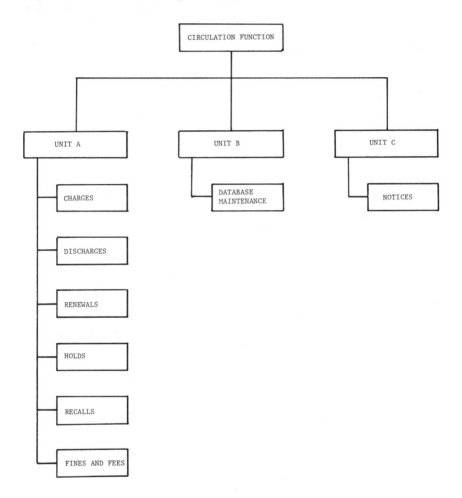

## The Physical Proximity of the Activities to Each Other

Activities that are physically housed close together can be managed more easily than those that are geographically separate. Geographically separate activities might be grouped in different units of the organizational structure.

## MANAGEMENT POSITIONS

Once the organizational units of an automated library function have been defined, the management positions needed can be identified. Several positions might be needed, including the function manager, unit managers, and first-line supervisors.

### The Function Manager

A position of chief administrator or manager of the automated library function must be established. This person will be responsible for the overall management of the function as an organizational unit of a department or division of the library. Specifically, the function manager will have several basic functions:

1. *Planning.* The function manager will decide what is to be done by setting goals and objectives for the function, in conjunction with others, and by identifying the appropriate courses of action necessary to accomplish the goals and objectives on long-range, medium-range, and short-range bases.
2. *Organizing.* The function manager will decide who is to do what in the function and delegate work to the function staff on that basis.
3. *Budgeting.* The function manager will decide what financial resources are necessary to achieve the goals and objectives established for the function.
4. *Staffing.* The function manager will be responsible for seeing that the work in the function is performed through the development of staff positions and the hiring of the most qualified people to fill the positions.
5. *Directing and Leading.* The function manager will provide leadership, guidance, and encouragement to the staff in their efforts to achieve the goals and objectives established for the function.
6. *Controlling.* The function manager will decide if the work of the staff is or is not getting done and what to do about it if it is not, through measurements and feedback established for the accomplishments of the staff.
7. *Coordinating.* The function manager will synchronize the efforts of the staff to make certain that the goals and objectives of the function are met in the most effective and efficient manner.
8. *Reporting.* The function manager will collect and convey statistics and other evaluative information about the function and its activities to others throughout the library.

## Unit Managers

If the automated library function is large, several other managerial positions will be necessary to assist the function manager. These assistant managers will be responsible for reporting to the function manager of one or more units of the function.

The responsibilities or functions of unit/program managers are the same as for the function manager, except on a smaller scale. The unit/program managers interpret and convert the instructions of the function manager into plans for accomplishing the work of their assigned areas of responsibility and assist the function manager by planning, organizing, budgeting, staffing, directing, controlling, coordinating, and reporting the activities within the function.

## First-Line Supervisors

When a unit of an automated function is large and must be divided into two or more smaller sections, additional managers may be needed. For example, the original cataloging unit of an automated cataloging function might be divided into several disciplines, with a supervisor responsible for each. The duties of this level of manager are to supervise the day-to-day work of a group of staff performing similar work, under direction of the unit manager. They might also assist the unit manager in planning, organizing, budgeting, staffing, directing, controlling, coordinating, and reporting the activities assigned to them.

## THE CHAIN OF COMMAND

The chain of command should be verified for the organizational units established for the automated library function. This will provide a foundation for developing staff positions for the function, as described in Chapter 5.

The chain of command will consist of a clear and unbroken line or "chain" of authority linking each staff member in the function with successively higher levels of authority. Orders or instructions and other formal communications should be conveyed from higher to lower levels of the function through this chain of command. Each staff member should understand to whom he or she reports and from whom to receive instructions and orders. To avoid delays and distortion in communications, the chain of command should be as short as possible. Bypassing the chain of command when issuing orders and instructions will confuse the employee and undermine the authority of the supervisor.

A corollary principle is that each person in the function should report to one and only one supervisor. This will avoid conflicts of orders and instructions and avoid uncertainty on the part of the individual employee. However, it may be desirable for a staff member to work in two or more units of an automated library function, either on a regular basis or occasionally. In this case, separate job descriptions should be prepared for the work in the separate units, and the employee should be informed from the beginning that more than one supervisor will be used. The supervisor and the employee should thoroughly understand that the staff member will report to only one supervisor at a time, depending upon the unit being worked in at the moment. As long as the split is well-planned and all those concerned understand the situation, no conflicts should arise.

## THE ADMINISTRATIVE GROUP

It is highly desirable that all managers within the automated library function be involved as much as possible in its overall management. To this end, a command, executive, or administrative team or group should be established for the automated function. Of concern should be the role, membership, and meetings of the administrative group.

### The Functions of the Administrative Group

The purposes or role of the administrative group for the automated function should be clearly established. The group should be informal and founded on the principles of decision sharing, mutual benefit and improvement in the morale of the unit managers, and the effectiveness and efficiency of the automated function.

The manager of the automated function still must be ultimately responsible and accountable for its successes and failures, but he or she can use the administrative group to learn the opinions of key staff, to solicit advice, and to generate ideas and act as a sounding board. The unit managers should use the opportunity to participate in the management of the function, contribute to its betterment, and add to their personal and professional growth and development.

Specifically, the administrative group can:

1. Formulate goals and objectives for the automated function as a whole.
2. Discuss problem areas in the function and consider possible solutions.
3. Discuss long-range, medium-range, and short-range plans for the function.
4. Coordinate activities of the function's organizational units.
5. Originate or discuss proposed policies for the function.

6. Discuss topics generated outside the function and formulate recommendations to be passed upward into the library organization.
7. Discuss budget plans.
8. Share progress reports of activities within the function.

## Membership of the Administrative Group

The membership of the administrative group should be well defined. The group might consist of the function manager and the managers of the function's units. The function manager should serve as the chair of the group. Other staff of the function or of other departments in the library can be invited to meet with the group from time to time as the need arises. If the automated function is small and no unit managers are necessary, then the staff as a whole can be considered as the administrative group.

## Meetings of the Administrative Group

When and how often the administrative group for the automated function will meet should be determined. The group should meet regularly, on at least a weekly basis. The meetings need not be lengthy, but it is important that a routine be set. A written agenda may be issued in advance of the meetings to make certain that specific topics are not forgotten and to enable the members to prepare themselves in advance, if necessary. If documents are to be discussed, copies should be distributed as far in advance of the meeting as possible to allow time for their study. The function manager should make it clear, however, that any additional topics can be brought up for discussion at the meetings.

Minutes of each meeting should be taken and distributed or routed to all staff of the function. The issues discussed and any conclusions or recommendations reached by the group should be reported. These minutes will be an important means of communicating information to the staff and to others outside the automated function.

## COMMUNICATIONS CHANNELS

In addition to the formal chain of command, other common communications channels should be established for the automated library function. The channels should be supported and used by managers on all levels within the function. Typical communications channels include regular staff meetings, newsletters, minutes of meetings, an open-door policy, visibility of managers and supervisors, a grievance procedure, a suggestion box, and exit interviews.

## Regular Staff Meetings

Conducting regular staff meetings is one of the most effective means of communication within the automated function. Staff meetings enable information to be conveyed from the function manager to the staff, provide an effective means for management to receive ideas and complaints from the staff, and provide a forum for the generation and discussion of ideas.

Meetings scheduled on a monthly basis should be adequate, with more frequent meetings when special circumstances warrant. A formal agenda may be issued as a reminder of special topics to be discussed or conveyed by the function manager to the staff. Sufficient time should be allowed for nonagenda topics and for other questions and answers. Brief minutes can be prepared and distributed as a record of the meetings.

## Newsletters

A newsletter can be an effective communications channel for circulating both formal and informal information to staff of the automated function. A single-sheet newsletter issued weekly or biweekly can be sufficient. A decision must be made whether it will be for official announcements and news only, informal news, or a combination of both.

Guidelines should be established for any newsletter issued, including its frequency, content, length, editor and other reporters, distribution, method of production, and cost.

## Minutes of Meetings

Distributing or routing the minutes of meetings of the function's administrative group and other committees to the staff of the automated function is a good means of disseminating information and keeping staff abreast of events. Minutes of groups outside the automated function also should be distributed or routed regularly.

## An Open-Door Policy

Another communications channel that should be made available to staff of the automated function is the open-door policy on the part of managers. Staff should feel free to walk into the office of the function manager and discuss a problem or seek advice on a job-related topic.

Care should be taken to stress to staff that an immediate supervisor should not ordinarily be by-passed in the process, except in extraordinary situations.

## Visibility of Managers and Supervisors

In addition to having an open-door policy, the function manager and other managers and supervisors should also make a point of stopping at the workstations of each staff member on a regular but unscheduled and informal basis. The purpose of these brief visits should be to make themselves more visible to the staff, to provide an opportunity for staff to ask questions of the managers, and to give the managers a feel for what work is being done.

## Grievance Procedures

The library as a whole should have a formal grievance procedure that staff of the automated function can use when they feel they have not received proper treatment by a supervisor. Staff should be able to register complaints against an individual or against the library and expect their grievances to be dealt with properly and fairly and in a timely manner.

## Suggestion Box

For those staff who might be too timid to offer suggestions or complaints to supervisors in person, a suggestion box can be placed in the automated function's quarters. Anonymous suggestions and complaints of a non-personal nature should be accepted. Each comment should be considered and answered by the function manager or delegated to another person to answer. The comments can be discussed by the administrative group at its regular meetings, and the answers to suggestions can be discussed at staff meetings, reported in a newsletter, or written out and posted on a staff bulletin board.

## Exit Interviews

Exit interviews can be an important channel for departing staff to convey information to managers within the automated function. A staff member leaving the function or the library often is willing to discuss potential problems and topics that he or she might otherwise be unwilling to discuss.

## COMMITTEES AND PROJECTS

The manager of the automated library function should always be seeking ways to include other staff in decision making and in the affairs of the function. To accomplish this, the manager should use committees and projects as extensively as possible.

### Committees

Committees can serve many useful purposes in the automated function. They provide a means of broadening the participation in decision making and of studying and handling specific problems within the function. Also, a committee may arrive at decisions that will be more satisfactory or acceptable than if they were made by the function manager alone.

Unless a committee is librarywide or interdepartmental, the function manager should appoint its members. A chair for a committee can also be selected by the function manager, or members can be allowed to choose their own leader. A purpose, charge, or set of responsibilities should be given the committee upon its inception.

Sometimes, a committee is expected to continue its existence over an extended period of time, from year to year. For example, committees in the function might be established for grievance procedures, issuing a newsletter, safety, and policies and procedures. In other cases, committees are organized to address a very specific problem or to complete a very specific task. Once the problem or task is solved or finished, the committee is dissolved. For example, a task force may be formed to conduct a search for a new staff member, to arrange a tour for a visiting dignitary, or to study the closing of the card catalog.

### Projects

Unlike a committee, a project is more elaborate and extensive. Substantial resources of the automated function may have to be allocated to a project in order for staff to complete its charge. For example, a project may be organized to convert the library's serial records to a machine-readable form, or to clear out a backlog of unprocessed materials. Staff time must be allocated over an extended period of time to complete the project. The staff assigned to a project may be relieved of other duties for the duration of the effort, or may be expected to work a portion of each day, week, or month on the project.

A project should be assigned a project manager, selected and appointed by the function manager. In addition, goals, objectives, constraints, a budget, and a timetable should be established for the undertaking.

## THE INFORMAL ORGANIZATION

The informal organization should not be overlooked in organizing and managing an automated library function. While the formal organization is concerned with positions and their place in the organizational structure, the informal organization is groups of staff drawn together informally by similar interests. For example, several staff members may regularly take coffee or lunch breaks together, or several staff may share rides to and from work. Informal groups may consist of staff from several departments or functions, or they may be from the automated function. Someone with power and authority in the formal organization may be just another friend in the informal organization.

The informal organization can be used as an effective communications channel in the automated function. Information usually is transmitted rapidly and efficiently over the grapevine, sometimes better than through formal channels. The greatest disadvantage to the grapevine is that information can sometimes be distorted when transmitted in this manner. The informal organization provides staff with a sense of belonging and security that tends to increase their job satisfaction; it serves as a safety valve for staff by giving them a forum for discussing and thus venting the frustrations that inevitably arise in any library function; and it serves as a useful communications channel for staff to learn about what is happening in the function and in the library as a whole.

The skilled manager understands the importance and usefulness of the informal organization. Since the informal organization cannot be eliminated, the good manager realizes that it serves a vital role in maintaining a healthy atmosphere in the function. The informal organization is a natural and beneficial part of any function and should not be considered a threat to either the formal organization or the individual managers in the function.

## FLEXIBILITY

Whatever organizational and management structure is developed for the automated library function should be flexible. The structures should be designed to be adapted easily to changing circumstances and situations. For example, during the building of an important online database, staff may be reassigned from several of the function's units to complete the project as rapidly as possible. When the urgency has passed and the work is completed, the staff can return to their usual duties. The organization and management structure of the automated function should never be an obstacle or barrier to achieving the purpose, goals, and objectives established for it.

## ADDITIONAL READINGS

*Advances in Library Administration and Organization.* Vol. 1-. Greenwich, CT: JAI Press, 1982-.

Broome, E.M. "Organizational Structures: An Outline." In *Aspects of Library Development Planning,* edited by J. Stephen Parker. New York: Mansell, 1983: 53-58.

Dale, Ernest. *Management: Theory and Practice.* 2nd ed. New York: McGraw-Hill, 1969.

Galbraith, Jay R. *Organization Design.* Reading: Addison-Wesley, 1977.

Gvishiani, Liudmila A. "Organizational Problems of Modern Library Management." *Libri* 31 (August 1981): 108-20.

Howard, Helen A. "Organizational Structure and Innovation in Academic Libraries." *College & Research Libraries* 42 (September 1981): 425-34.

Katz, Daniel, and Robert L. Kahn. *The Social Psychology of Organizations.* 2nd ed. New York: Wiley, 1978.

Lee, Sul H. *Emerging Trends in Library Organization: What Influences Change.* Ann Arbor, MI: Pierian Press, 1978.

Levy, Amir, and Uri Merry. *Organizational Transformation: Approaches, Strategies, Theories.* New York: Praeger, 1986.

Lynch, Beverly, ed. *Management Strategies for Libraries: A Basic Reader.* New York: Neal-Schuman, 1985.

Martin, Lowell A. *Organizational Structure of Libraries.* New York: Scarecrow Press, 1984.

Schermerhorn, John R. *Management for Productivity.* 2nd ed. New York: Wiley, 1986.

Shaughnessy, Thomas W. "Technology and the Structure of Libraries." *Libri* 32 (June 1982): 149-55.

Sisk, Henry L. *Management & Organization.* 3rd ed. Cincinnati: South-Western Publishing Company, 1977.

Stevens, Norman D. *Communication Throughout Libraries.* Metuchen, NJ: Scarecrow Press, 1983.

Taylor, Frederick W. *The Principles of Scientific Management.* New York: Norton, 1967.

White, Don A., and T.D. Wilson. "Relevance of Theory and a New Approach to Library Structure." *Libri* 34 (September 1984): 175-85.

# Chapter 4
# Tasks and Procedures

The separation of the automated library function into its component activities was completed as organizational and management structures for the function were developed in Chapter 3. Tasks comprising each activity of the automated function now must be identified and procedures designed for each of the tasks. Since the automated function will require different procedures from the manual function it replaces, it usually is not necessary or desirable to study existing processing methods and compare them to the new function. As a matter of fact, it may be desirable to ignore the old routines entirely during the design of procedures for the automated function in order to ensure a fresh approach.

The purpose of this chapter is to discuss the design of the preferred method of performing the work of an automated library function. Specifically, its topics include:

- Task identification
- Procedures design
- Documentation of procedures
- Testing procedures

## TASK IDENTIFICATION

The first step of designing procedures for an automated library function might be to identify the tasks comprising each of its activities.

A *task* is defined as a group of related operations performed on an input of information, materials, or other items necessary to provide or yield a desired outcome or output.

The purpose of an activity can serve as a focal point for identifying its component tasks. This purpose will indicate what the activity will be attempting to do, either produce a product or provide a service.

*Example*: The purpose of the Borrower Record Update Activity is to add, delete, or correct information within records in the Borrower File.

The component tasks of an activity are derived from its purpose. The documentation supplied by the designer of the software supporting the automated function can be used as a guide in this process. Also, the librarian's professional knowledge, experience, and imagination will be helpful. To illustrate the process, the typical tasks of typical activities of an automated circulation function are shown in Figure 4-1.

**FIGURE 4-1. Typical Tasks of an Automated Circulation Function**

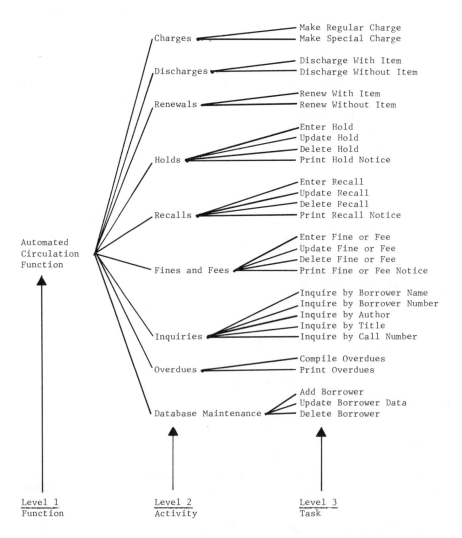

## PROCEDURES DESIGN

When a task is performed, a *procedure* is followed. A procedure is the preferred method of performing the processing operations or tasks on the input of information, materials, or other items necessary to produce the output. The staff and the computer supporting the automated function follow the procedures as they perform their share of the work in the function.

Designing procedures is an iterative process, in that a procedure must be developed separately for each task. The result of this process will be sets of procedures that the staff and the computer will follow as an activity is operated. The procedures established for the automated library function will be used to design jobs for the people who will perform the work in the function and for incorporation in a procedures manual to be used as a training and reference guide for operating the function.

Elements of a procedure include task output, task input, processing operations, processing sequence, and processing decisions. A schematic model of a procedure is shown in Figure 4-2.

### Task Output

The outcome, end result, or output of the task, which can be either a product or a service, must be specified.

*Example*: Output of the Charging or Check-Out Task is a record of a loan made to a borrower in good standing, filed into the Circulation Transaction File.

*Example*: Output of the Inquire by Author Task is a display of a record associated with an author's name used as a search argument against the file.

Each task should have one and only one clearly-defined output. When more than one output is identified, two or more tasks usually have been inadvertently combined and must be separated, or, the correct output may not yet have been properly identified.

All other elements of the task—input, operations, sequence, and decisions—are directed toward producing or yielding this singular end result or outcome.

### Task Input

Once the output of a task has been defined, the "raw material" or input needed to produce the desired outcome can be identified. Most library procedures require a combination of verbal or recorded information and physical items as input. Physical items such as a book or an identification card can be considered input to processing, al-

**FIGURE 4-2. A Model of a Procedure**

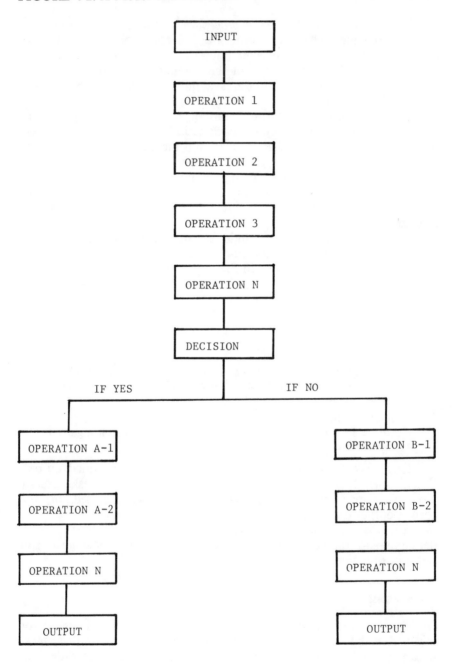

though only the information describing or representing these objects stored in the barcodes will be processed, not the objects themselves.

*Example*: Input for the Charging or Check-Out Task is borrowers' identification badges containing barcodes, books and other materials containing barcodes, and the current date and time.

*Example*: Input to the Prepare Labels Task is blank labels and a computer display of the information to be placed on the labels.

The computer itself accepts information as input, and that information must be in a form acceptable to it, i.e., machine-readable form.

## Processing Operations

The processing or operations needed to convert the input of information and/or physical items into the desired output, the sequence in which the operations will be performed, and any decisions that must be made as operations are performed must be determined.

An *operation* is a unit of work assigned to a person or the computer supporting the automated function. The input to the procedures is converted to output as these step-by-step operations are performed. Common processing operations include interviewing, recording, verification, classification, summarization, dissemination, sorting, calculating, filing or storage, retrieving, duplicating, transporting, opening, closing, gathering, cutting, lifting, removing, turning, and many others. These operations are performed repeatedly during processing on the input of information and/or physical items to achieve the desired outcome.

The specific operations to be performed as a procedure is followed should be identified. Again, the documentation supplied by the designer or vendor of the software supporting the automated function can be a starting point in this process, supplemented by the librarian's professional knowledge, experience, and logical thinking.

The operations should consist of a verb, which specifies the action to be taken, and a noun, which specifies the information, materials, or other item to be acted upon. To illustrate this, some common processing operations are shown in the table in Figure 4-3.

In the automated function, humans and the computer share the responsibility for performing the operations. A person might perform the first four processing operations; a computer, the next three operations; a person, the next two operations; and so on, until the job is completed. The computer cannot perform direct physical acts, although it can be used to control other machines that perform physical operations. Physical operations such as moving, inserting, pasting, opening, closing, gathering, cutting, lifting, removing, turning, and so on, must be performed by humans or machines other than the computer.

**FIGURE 4-3. Common Processing Operations**

| | |
|---|---|
| INTERVIEW USERS | DUPLICATE ADDRESSES |
| RECORD SELECTIONS | TRANSPORT TRUCKS |
| VERIFY TITLES | OPEN BOOKS |
| CLASSIFY REQUESTS | CLOSE FOLDERS |
| SUMMARIZE DATA | GATHER SHEETS |
| DISSEMINATE MEMOS | CUT LABELS |
| SORT FORMS | LIFT BOXES |
| CALCULATE FINES | REMOVE CONTENTS |
| FILE REPORTS | TURN KNOBS |
| RETRIEVE NAMES | |

## Processing Sequence

The operations in a procedure must be performed in a preferred sequence to ensure that the efficiency of both staff and the computer are optimized, while not compromising the outcome or quality of service to library users. The movement of input through the processing steps is referred to as *workflow*.

In a manual function, staff might have a wide variance in the sequence in which operations could be performed, while still achieving the desired outcome of the work. Some variance in performing processing operations by staff can be tolerated in an automated function, but the computer itself does not—can not—deviate from its programmed paths, except in clearly-defined instances. The sequence of performing operations should be logical and as efficient as possible.

## Processing Decisions

Decisions may be required as the processing operations are performed in their specified sequence. Depending on the result of a decision being made, alternate sequences of operations will be required. For example, if during the charging of an item the computer detected that the borrower owed a large fine, a decision must be made by either the software or a staff member whether or not to continue with the charge. If the answer is not to continue, then one set of operations must be performed. If the answer is to let the borrower check out the item, then another sequence must be followed. These decisions and the resulting diverging paths in processing operations must be foreseen in advance and incorporated into the workflow.

## DOCUMENTATION OF PROCEDURES

Several tools are available to assist in the design of procedures and in the documentation process. One of the best tools is the decision flowchart, sometimes referred to as a logic or system flowchart.

The decision flowchart is a graphic or pictorial representation of the sequence of operations performed on information and/or physical items as they move through a system. This type of chart depicts all inputs, processing operations, the sequence of the operations, decisions made in the workflow and the alternative courses of action to be taken as a result of those decisions, and the output of a system. In essence, it depicts the workflow through the system.

The charts are useful as aids in visualizing the elements of the workflow and the sequence of the processing operations during the work design activity. They also can become a part of the procedures manual for reference purposes and for training the staff to perform their jobs in the system. Since this type of chart is widely used and understood in systems work, it can be an excellent medium of communication with others who wish to understand the automated function.

A decision flowchart is constructed by stringing together symbols that have been standardized by the American National Standards Association to represent input and output, processing operations, and decisions. Concise annotations are written inside each symbol to describe what input and output, processing operations, and decisions are represented in the system. Nouns are used in input and output symbols, verbs in processing symbols, and questions for decisions.

Flowlines connect the symbols in a chart, with arrowheads indicating the direction of the workflow. These and several other symbols, such as the start/delay/end, page connector, and annotation symbols, will be sufficient for the librarian to construct adequate flowcharts. The set of symbols is shown in Figure 4-4. The charting begins at the top of a page and progresses downwards. The connector symbol is used as a guide from page to page of the chart. A template is available to facilitate flowchart preparation. Software packages for flowcharting on a computer also are available.

Flowcharting can begin with an examination of other examples of charts in this and other books and articles. The chart can be started with a simple representation of the system, using broadly-stated operations (see Figure 4-5). Then, each of the broad operations is divided into smaller steps. The process is repeated until sufficient detail is shown.

Operations to be performed both by staff and the computer are included. When a decision is necessary in the workflow, a decision symbol with a "yes" flow emerging from one point of the symbol block and a "no" flow from another is inserted. Processing is thus broken into two diverging sequences of operations resulting when either path is

## FIGURE 4-4. Standard Flowcharting Symbols

BEGIN, END        Denotes a start, stop, delay, or interruption
in the flow of work.

PROCESSING        Denotes any operation performed to convert
input into output.

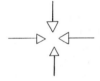

DECISION          Denotes any decision whose outcome results in
separate processing paths being taken.

INPUT OR
OUTPUT            Denotes data, forms, materials, or other items
to be processed.  Also denotes processed data,
forms, etc., as output.

Denotes the sequence and direction of flow in the
chart.  Also connects symbols.

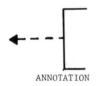

Denotes additional comments or a clarification
thought necessary.

ANNOTATION

Denotes exit or entry from another part of a
chart.  Also connects pages.

CONNECTOR

followed. The main flow of work consists of the processing operations
and decisions that occur normally in a procedure; the alternative
processing operations and decisions represent the exceptions to the

**FIGURE 4-5. A Simple Representation of an Automated Function, Using Broadly Stated Operations**

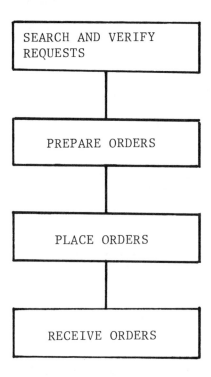

norm. Part of a flowchart for processing in Charging or Check-Out in an automated circulation function is shown in Figure 4-6.

## TESTING PROCEDURES

After the preferred procedure has been designed preliminarily for a task, the workflow should be tested to validate the procedure's acceptability and workability. The test results may indicate flaws in the initial design of a procedure, point out necessary steps overlooked in the design process, indicate unnecessary steps that could be omitted, indicate operations that should be expanded, or indicate steps that are not in proper sequence. A redesign of all or parts of the procedure may be subsequently required.

This process—test, redesign, retest, redesign—may have to be repeated several times before a procedure seems adequate. Even then, when the automated function is placed in operation, more flaws may be discovered. Some flaws in a procedure may not be readily apparent until the automated function has been in operation for a period of

**FIGURE 4-6. Part of a Decision Flowchart for Charging in an Automated Circulation Function**

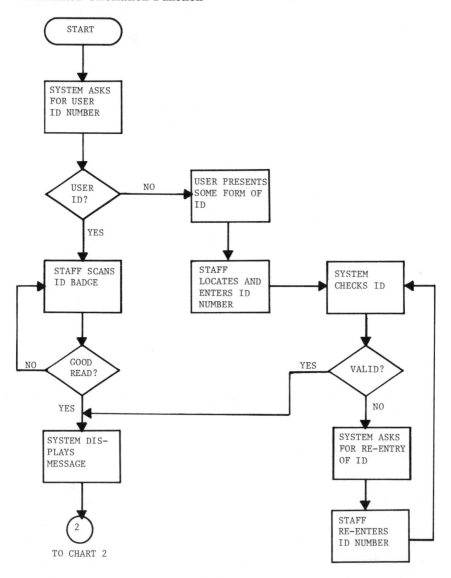

time. A procedure should never be considered perfect or complete and frozen forever; it should be under constant review for better and simpler means of accomplishing the activity's goal.

The preliminary procedure design, which should be tested using the software of the automated function itself, can have several steps. Of concern should be test site preparation, building test files, assembling test input items, staff preparation, testing procedures, and redesigning procedures.

## Test Site Preparation

A site simulating as nearly as possible the environment of the activity should be prepared for testing its procedure. Furniture with workspace similar to that anticipated for the automated function should be in place. The computer terminal or terminals needed should be installed and tested as fully operational. Software to be used should be in a test mode and available for use.

## Building Test Files

One or more test files may have to be created in computer storage before a procedure can be tested. Test records should be entered into storage, detected errors corrected, and any essential indexes generated. For example, to test the Charge Activity of an automated circulation function, several records should be entered in a test borrower file. Some of the records should be normal, but others should have, for example, an excessive amount of fines, a stolen identification badge reported, a large number of items charged out, and the like. This will allow full testing of the activity under workaday conditions where a wide variety of situations arise.

## Assembling Test Input Items

Test materials, such as blank forms, forms with appropriate test information, identification badges, labels, books, and other items, should be gathered, inventoried, and placed in position for the test. For example, several borrower badges matching records in the test borrower file and books with barcodes matching records in the test bibliographic file should be gathered.

## Staff Preparation

Staff must be trained for the test. Full documentation of the procedures need not be ready at this time; the test may be conducted using only drafts of flowcharts. Full documentation can be completed later. The librarian may give the staff who will perform the test only a general overview of what will happen, then explain each operation, one at a time, as it is performed in the test mode.

The staff who will perform the operations in test mode should be briefed fully on the operations to be performed and their sequence. It is best to use for the test the same staff who probably will be performing the work when the system is "live."

## Testing Procedures

With the workplace simulating the environment of the real automated function and the test files and the test input items assembled and ready, the procedure can be tested for weaknesses in the design. At the start, speed is not of great importance. The operations should be performed slowly at first so that the process can be observed by the staff. All the operations in a procedure should be tested as thoroughly as possible, under as many conditions as possible.

Once it has been verified that the operations are correct and working well, the entire flow should be tested to ascertain that the software and the staff function together smoothly and to detect any incompatibilities.

The designer of the procedure should be taking notes so that the workflow can later be revised. Some designers like to modify the procedures by altering the decision flowcharts or flow process charts as the test progresses, while others prefer to take notes during the tests and redraft the flowcharts later.

## Redesigning Procedures

The test results may indicate that the processing operations, sequence, and decisions are adequate and workable as designed, or results may show that redesign of the procedure is required. If redesign is indicated, modifications to the flowcharts are made and the design is tested again to validate the corrections or changes. The process of testing-redesign-retesting-redesign may have to be repeated several times until an acceptable procedure is established.

## ADDITIONAL READINGS

American National Standard, Industrial Engineering Terminology. *Work Measurement and Methods (Z94.12-1972)*. New York: American Society of Mechanical Engineers, 1973.

American National Standards Association. *Standard Flowchart Symbols and Their Use in Information Processing (X3.5)*. New York, [Use latest edition].

Barnes, Ralph M. *Motion and Time Study: Design and Measurement of Work.* 6th ed. New York: Wiley, 1968.

Bolles, Shirley W. "Use of Flow Charts in the Analysis of Library Operations." *Special Libraries* 58 (February 1967): 95-98.

Corbin, John. *Managing the Library Automation Project*. Phoenix: Oryx Press, 1985.

Dougherty, Richard M., and Fred J. Heinritz. *Scientific Management of Library Operations.* 2nd ed. New York: Scarecrow Press, 1982.

Gilchrist, Alan. "Further Comments on the Terminology of the Analysis of Library Systems." *Aslib Proceedings* 20 (October 1968): 408-12.

Heinritz, Fred J. "Analysis and Evaluation of Current Library Procedures." *Library Trends* 21 (April 1973): 522-32.

Hopeman, Richard J. *Production: Concepts, Analysis, Control.* Columbus, OH: Charles E. Merrill Books, 1965.

Maynard, Harold B., ed. *Industrial Engineering Handbook.* 3rd ed. New York: McGraw-Hill, 1971.

Nadler, Gerald. *Work Design: A Systems Concept.* Rev. ed. Homewood: Irwin, 1970.

Pilitsis, John V. "Analysis and Design Techniques for Information Processing Systems." In *Handbook of Industrial Engineering,* edited by Gavriel Salvendy. New York: Wiley, 1982: 12.4.1-19.

Thomas, P.A. *Task Analysis of Library Operations.* (Aslib Occasional Publication No. 8). London: Aslib, 1971.

Thomas, P.A., and H. East. "Comments on the Terminology of the Analysis and the Functions of Forms Therein." *Aslib Proceedings* 20 (August 1968): 340-44.

# Chapter 5
# Job Design and Staffing

Staff will be the most valuable asset of the automated library function. The software and hardware supporting the function may be the best available. But without a well-selected and well-trained staff, automation cannot be used effectively in the library, since the success of automated functions depends to a great extent upon the quality of staff and their well being and motivation as they perform their share of work. In this chapter, some critical aspects of job design and staffing are discussed. The topics include:

- Job revision for the automated function
- Determination of positions needed
- Introducing change
- Staffing the automated function
- Performance standards
- Education and training of staff

## JOB REVISION FOR THE AUTOMATED FUNCTION

A first step of staffing the automated library function should be to revise all job descriptions. The duties and responsibilities of the existing staff must be redefined to reflect the work to be done in the automated function.

Changes in staff duties and responsibilities are inevitable when an automated function is implemented. The extent of the changes will depend upon:

1. The nature of the function being automated.
2. The amount of automation being introduced.
3. The extent to which existing activities will be streamlined.
4. The imaginative uses of staff considered possible by the function's management.

Some staff may have only a few new or changed duties and responsibilities, while others may find their jobs radically different. A team consisting of the manager of the automated function, other unit managers, and other supervisors as needed should be responsible for revising the jobs for the function.

The team might take several steps in revising jobs for the automated function.

## Analyzing and Ranking Tasks of the Automated Function

The first step of revising jobs should be to analyze and rank the tasks of the automated function. The set of tasks should be analyzed and ranked on the basis of their complexity and difficulty. The purpose of this step is to lay the foundation for determining which tasks should be assigned to the various jobs. The tasks comprising an automated function were identified in Chapter 4.

To facilitate the analysis and ranking, each task can be placed on a card which can be easily rearranged during the deliberations by the team. While analyzing and ranking the tasks comprising the automated function, the team should keep several considerations in mind, including:

1. Skills and skill levels required for an individual to perform a task effectively (no skills, some skills, high skills).
2. Special knowledge and knowledge level required (none, some, moderate, high technology).
3. End responsibilities involved (little, moderate, great).
4. Difficulty of the task (simple, routine, varied, complex).
5. Repetitiveness of the task (highly repetitive, repeated infrequently).
6. Experience required (none, some, a lot).
7. Judgment required (none, limited, shared, independent).

The most complex and difficult tasks should be placed at the top of the list, and the simplest, at the bottom. The higher the skills, knowledge, and end responsibilities required for someone to perform a task, the higher it should be placed in the list. The ranked tasks also should be tentatively separated into levels that correspond to the grade levels within the classification system used by the library.

When many tasks are to be ranked, it might be wise for each manager within the function to rank the tasks of his or her own unit. The unit rankings can later be compared to make certain that comparable tasks are given the same position in all groupings. Discrepancies can be resolved through discussions.

Figure 5-1 shows a set of unranked tasks for an automated cataloging system and the same set after the tasks have been analyzed and organized according to complexity and difficulty, arranged in rank order, and grouped into tentative grade levels.

## FIGURE 5-1. A Set of Tasks for an Automated Cataloging Function, Before and After Ranking

Before Ranking

```
Search titles in OCLC
Evaluate the work of staff
Fire staff members when necessary
Locate matches to materials in-hand in OCLC database
Compare OCLC online records to materials in-hand
Insert edited records into "save" file for review
Counsel staff members on tardiness
Prepare work schedules for staff
Review and approve edited records in "save" file
Catalog materials not located in OCLC
Search material not found in OCLC in other bibliographic tools
Produce on records in "save" file after review
Tag data elements for input
Input records for materials cataloged originally
Review and approve authority records
Resolve conflicts in authority records
Compile statistics for all staff activities into monthly reports
Write monthly reports of system activities
Train new staff members to edit OCLC records
Provide direct supervision to staff on day-to-day basis
Prepare budget requests for the function
Prepare long-range plans for the function
Maintain documentation for the function
Enter corrections online into local records
```

After Ranking

Job 1

```
Train new staff members to edit OCLC records
Provide direct supervision to staff on day-to-day basis
Prepare budget requests for the function
Prepare long-range plans for the function
Prepare work schedules for staff
Counsel staff members on tardiness
Fire staff members when necessary
Evaluate the work of staff
```

Job 2

```
Catalog materials not located in OCLC
Tag data elements for input
Review and approve edited records in "save" file
Review and approve authority records
Resolve conflicts in authority records
```

Job 3

```
Search titles in OCLC
Locate matches to materials in-hand in OCLC database
Compare OCLC online records to materials in-hand
Edit OCLC online records to match materials in-hand
Insert edited records into "save" file for review
Produce on records in "save" file after review
```

Job 4

```
Search materials not found in OCLC in other bibliographic tools
Compile statistics for all staff activities into monthly reports
Maintain documentation for the function
Enter corrections online into local records
```

## Designing Jobs for the Automated Function

The jobs for the automated library function should be designed by using the results of the task analysis and ranking. It should be remembered that a job is a set of tasks grouped together to form the workload of an individual.

When designing the jobs, the team should keep the following in mind:

1. The duties and responsibilities for a job should be as closely related as possible.
2. However, the duties and responsibilities assigned to a job should be as varied and challenging as possible.

Care should be taken that the relationship between jobs within the function is clear. There should be no overlap or gaps in responsibilities. Also, some flexibility of duties and responsibilities among staff in the automated function is desirable. For example, should the computer supporting a function be inoperable and the staff cannot perform their regular duties, they should be able to move rapidly to others until they can return to performing their primary duties.

## Revising Existing Job Descriptions

Once the tasks comprising the activities of the automated function have been analyzed and ranked according to their difficulty and complexity, grouped into grade levels, and organized into jobs, the existing job descriptions should be reviewed and revised. New tasks must replace those from the existing function that have become obsolete.

The duties and responsibilities for some jobs may be the same in both the existing function and in the automated function, while some existing duties and responsibilities may be completely replaced with new ones. In some cases, the duties and responsibilities for a job will remain the same in the automated function, but must be performed in a different sequence or from a different perspective.

Some guidelines can be offered for revising job descriptions for the automated function:

1. The job description should contain, as a minimum, the job title, the job summary, the work performed, the relationship to other jobs in the function, special qualifications for the job, and special information.
2. Wording in the job description should be clear and simple.
3. Action verbs followed by nouns for things acted upon should be used to describe duties and responsibilities. A telegraphic style should be used. Unimportant words such as "a," "and," and "of" are used only to improve concepts. For example, "assigns fund codes," or "keys borrower information into storage."

4. The terminology used to describe work, job titles, etc., should be standardized from one job description to another.

Care should be taken to revise the minimum education and skill requirements to appropriate levels to reflect the new duties and responsibilities.

A sample job description for a support position in an automated acquisitions system is shown in Figure 5-2.

**FIGURE 5-2. A Sample Job Description for a Support Position in an Automated Acquisitions Function**

```
Title:              Library Assistant
Classification:     O&C 5
Position:           1-1-39289-002
Department:         Acquisitions
Reports to:         Manager, Monograph Ordering
Incumbent:          Grizelda Smith
```

GENERAL FUNCTION

Performs a variety of duties surrounding the input, maintenance, and receiving of titles on order.

DUTIES

1. Inputs and updates purchase requests in the Geac Acquisitions System and authorizes purchase requests for ordering (30%).

2. Receives books in the system, approves invoices for payment, and prepares books for forwarding to Bibliographic Control for cataloging (30%).

3. Searches online database (Geac) to determine library holdings for purchase requests and approval books (15%).

4. Communicates orally and in writing with vendors regarding claims, cancellations, incomplete shipments, and returns (10%).

5. Searches traditional bibliographic sources (approval microfiche, Books in Print, etc.) for holdings and availability data for purchase requests (5%).

6. Checks approval books against invoices as they are received and arranges approval shipments for review by librarians (5%).

7. Performs related duties as required (5%).

SUPERVISION

Received: Closely supervised by the program manager with frequent consultations and direction.
Given: None.

MINIMUM QUALIFICATIONS

Education/Experience: High school diploma or equivalent; one year of college and one year of relevant work experience; or an equivalent combination of education.
Skills/Abilities: Ability to type minimum of 35 wpm with 5 or fewer errors; accuracy and attention to detail essential; reading knowledge of foreign language helpful.

## Writing New Job Descriptions If Necessary

When entirely new jobs must be created for the automated library function, completely new job descriptions must be written. These should be written in accordance with the practices of the library, in conjunction with the considerations discussed above.

## Gaining Approval of the Revised and New Job Descriptions

Formal review and approval of revised and new job descriptions must be obtained. The chain of command within the library should be followed in obtaining this approval.

The library's top management staff will be concerned that the job descriptions are compatible with others in the library, to make certain that inequities between functions and departments have not resulted.

Approval of the job descriptions by the personnel department within the library's host institution also must be gained in most instances. This office will be concerned with compatibility of the revised and new job descriptions with those elsewhere within the host institution and with the existing personnel classification system.

## DETERMINATION OF POSITIONS NEEDED

The next step in this process might be to determine the number of positions needed for an automated library function. Several staff may be performing the same job in a function, using the same job description. Individual people will fill positions, which are defined as collections of tasks and responsibilities that make up the total work load of those people.

An automated library function may have the same number of jobs as the previous manual function, but may require fewer staff positions than before. Or the automated function may require fewer jobs but more staff than before. The number of staff positions needed for the automated function will depend upon:

1. The nature of the automated function.
2. The number of activities in the function.
3. The volume of work in the function.

## INTRODUCING THE STAFF TO CHANGE

Successful integration of automation into a library function will mean radical changes in procedures, workstations, jobs, management, and many other aspects of existing routines and perhaps in the social structure of an existing function. However, change is feared by many library staff members. The astute librarian will recognize that fear of change can result in resistance to the implementation of automation. Therefore, a strategy for introducing the staff to change is needed as a prelude to initiating the automation project, to minimize the problems of staff resistance to the new ideas accompanying the integration of automation into a function.

Change can be introduced to staff in a number of ways, including initiating an education program, involving staff in the automation project, apprising staff fully of automation plans, apprising staff of their roles in the automated function, and introducing change a little at a time.

## Initiating an Education Program

One way of removing some of the fear of machines and technology and the changes they bring is to educate the staff about these things, on the theory that the more people know about the things they fear, the less they will fear them. The education also would give staff a better insight to their jobs, enable them to give better service to the public, and make them better employees in general. A broad understanding of automation's options can lead to the most effective means of both coping with the challenges and making the most of new opportunities. Staff orientation and training for automation is further discussed below.

## Involving Staff in the Automation Project

Another critical factor to making the automation project a success will be staff involvement. The ultimate success of an automated function depends to a great extent upon the support and interest of the staff who operate and manage it. Therefore, the staff should be involved extensively in the integration of automation into a function. They will be more prone to accept automation if they feel personally involved in its implementation and if they can see tangible benefits to themselves and to the library. An automated function imposed upon the rank and file staff without their prior knowledge or involvement may not be readily or easily accepted.

Staff involvement ideally should have begun as requirements for automation were being developed, during the system acquisition stage of the undertaking. If this was not possible, then staff involvement should begin early in the implementation process. The best way of involving staff in the process is to assign responsibility for completing the various steps to key staff and to use committees or task forces as extensively as possible during the project. This can ensure broad contributions and full consideration of ideas from all sources.

## Apprising Staff Fully of Automation Plans

Staff should be apprised fully of plans to automate a function. This process should begin as soon as the decision is made to automate. They should be kept apprised of progress being made in the automation plan on an ongoing basis. Without effective, frequent communication, the implementation process could be severely impaired. Communication is needed for alerting staff about the latest status of aspects of the implementation and for exchanging information about issues and concerns.

## Apprising Staff of Their Roles in the Automated Function

In addition to fearing change itself, staff also fear that there will be no place for them in the automated function or that they will not be able to master new duties and responsibilities assigned to them. Also, a lack of continued assurance during the integration process can be a major shortcoming of the effort, since imaginations often run rampant as reports are heard that other institutions are dismissing staff as a result of automation.

Staff should be apprised early in the automation program that they will be involved in the planning and integration process, that they will be retrained thoroughly for new duties and responsibilities, and that they will be given an opportunity to learn more about computers and related technology as the program unfolds.

## Introducing Change a Little at a Time

Finally, it is always a good idea to introduce change slowly, a little at a time, to give staff time to adjust to the changes more easily and readily. Change introduced gradually can make the implementation of a radically different automated function more palatable to the staff.

## STAFFING THE AUTOMATED FUNCTION

Once the jobs required for the automated library function have been defined, their job descriptions have been revised or written, and the number of positions needed has been determined, the function must be staffed. If all existing staff are to be utilized in the automated function, this step might be as simple as informing the individuals of their new duties and responsibilities. But in some cases, current staff may not be able to handle duties in the automated function. For example, while card filers were needed in the manual function, online data entry operators may be required in the automated function. Staff numbers may vary; the automated function may require fewer or even more staff than did the manual function.

In staffing the automated function, several steps might be taken.

## Developing a Staffing Plan

Before staff are informed of their new roles, if any, within the automated function, a staffing plan should be developed. This plan should include:

1. Which individuals will fill specific positions.
2. Which individuals, if any, must be transferred or terminated.
3. Which positions, if any, must be filled with new staff.

## Meeting with All Staff

After the staffing plan has been devised and before individuals are told their new duties and responsibilities, a meeting of all staff should be held. The purposes of this meeting are to:

1. Explain generally to all staff the staffing needs of the automated function.
2. Answer frankly and honestly any general questions from the staff regarding the staffing needs of the automated function.

Specific assignments in the automated function should not be discussed at this time. The staff's continued importance to the library and to the automated function should be stressed. Assurances that the staff will be trained for their new assignments should also be given.

## Conducting Individual Staff Conferences

After the general meeting with all staff, individual conferences with each staff member should be held, so that the function's manager can personally inform each person of his or her role in the automated function. Staff may have to be told:

1. Their new duties and responsibilities in the automated function; or
2. That they will be transferred to other units of the library; or
3. That, as a last resort, they must be terminated.

A copy of his or her new job description should be given to each staff member who will be continuing in the automated function. After staff have had a chance to study their revised job descriptions, a second conference should be held with each individual to answer additional questions or to provide further assurances that each person will be thoroughly retrained for his or her new duties and responsibilities.

It may be necessary to eliminate some staff positions entirely when an automated function is implemented. Certainly, positions should not be retained when a function is automated unless sufficient work is available for these staff. Cost savings through automation will come primarily through a better utilization of existing staff and a reduction in staff when necessary. Most libraries simply transfer excess staff from the function being automated to other organizational units of the library or possibly outside the library in other parts of the library's host institution. Thus, while there will be a reduction of staff within the function upon its automation, the number of staff in the library overall might remain the same. Selection of the staff to be transferred might depend upon:

1. Whether or not the individual's skills and abilities are needed in the automated function.
2. His or her seniority in the function.
3. His or her desire for a transfer.

In some cases, the library can reduce staff in a function being automated through attrition. That is, when a staff member resigns or retires, the person is not replaced and the position is dissolved or transferred to another area of the library. This option is always preferable to staff terminations.

As a last resort, the library may have to terminate some staff not needed in an automated function. This step should be taken only if:

1. No duties and responsibilities for an individual can be identified within the automated function; or
2. The individual cannot be transferred to another unit of the library; or
3. A position cannot be eliminated through attrition.

## Hiring Additional Staff If Necessary

In some cases, new staff must be hired for the automated function, perhaps because new positions were created, or because there were vacant positions as the function was being automated.

Qualified staff elsewhere in the library organization should be given the opportunity to apply for vacant positions in the automated function. Internal candidates are already known to other managers who can provide in-depth appraisals of them, thus reducing the risks of hiring individuals who may later prove to be poor choices. Filling positions from within also improves morale throughout the library, because other staff can see that they too may later be considered for promotions, given their good performance. However, internal candidates can foster organizational inbreeding.

At least some positions should be filled by outsiders who can bring fresh insights and perspectives into the function. While hiring outsiders will take longer and cost more, it may be best in the long run for the automated function.

## PERFORMANCE STANDARDS

Another step of job design and staffing for an automated library function might be to establish performance standards for staff working in the function.

A performance standard is a measure of the expected output of an average employee for a period of time such as an hour, a day, a week, or a month. Performance standards can be used in a number of ways in the automated function, including:

1. Providing goals for which staff can strive. It is generally known that staff will respond better when goals are readily known and seem to be actually attainable.
2. Identifying those staff who may need additional training. Staff who continually fail to achieve the expected output may need additional training or discipline.
3. Identifying staff for promotions, merit pay, or other recognition. Staff who consistently exceed the work standards should be recognized and praised by management.

If performance standards for the automated function are to be established, several steps might be taken.

### Determining Appropriate Areas for Performance Standards

The work where performance standards will be appropriate should be determined. Standards can be established for most production-type activities where a steady flow of work is available and output can be measured. However, when work is dependent upon random activities, such as at reference or circulation desks, standards are not useful because staff have no control over the flow of work. Examples of some performance standards can be found in Figure 5-3.

### Appointing Teams to Set the Standards

It is important that those people who will be affected by performance standards be allowed to set them. To accomplish this, teams can be established to set standards in the identified areas of the automated function. For example, one team can be established to set cataloging

**FIGURE 5-3. Examples of Performance Standards**

| Standard | | Hourly Goal | Monthly Goal |
|---|---|---|---|
| Acquisitions: | Titles Received | 20 Titles | 2400-2700 Titles |
| Acquisitions: | Titles Ordered | 20 Titles | 2200-2500 Titles |
| Acquisitions: | Titles Paid | 45 Titles | 4900-5600 Titles |
| Acquisitions: | Pre-Order Verification | 50 Titles | 5000-5200 Titles |
| Acquisitions: | Maintain Voucher File | 90 Vouchers | 6000-6500 Vouchers |
| Acquisitions: | Renew Serial Titles | 2 Titles | 234 Titles |
| Cataloging: | DLC Cataloging | 5-7 Titles | 800-1100 Titles |
| Cataloging: | Member Cataloging | 5-6 Titles | 800-1100 Titles |
| Cataloging: | Added Copies Added | 12-16 Copies | 2000-2600 Copies |
| Cataloging: | Added Volumes Added | 4-5 Volumes | 600-800 Volumes |
| Cataloging: | Cataloging at Terminal | 10-15 Titles | 400-600 Titles |
| Cataloging: | Searching | 15-40 Titles | 2400-6400 Titles |
| Cataloging: | Input Edited Workforms | 15-20 Forms | 2400-3200 Forms |

output standards, another team for serials check in standards, another team for standards for the number of acquisition requests that can be keyed into storage, and so on.

It is important that a few guidelines be established for the team to follow in setting performance standards:

1. The standards should not be too low. If standards are set too low, many staff can exceed them rapidly and incentives are diminished.
2. The standards should not be too high. When no one can meet the standards, staff become discouraged and stop trying to achieve them.
3. The standards should be set for an "average" worker.

There are several ways the teams can set performance standards, including:

1. Estimating acceptable performance levels based upon the past experiences of the team members in their areas of expertise.
2. Gathering statistical data on the past performance of a number of employees. The average output can then be determined and accepted as a performance standard.
3. Conducting time studies for the areas under consideration for standards. The average of a number of units of work performed can be used as the performance standard.

## Trying the Standards

After performance standards have been established for work in the automated function, the staff should try them for a period of time, such as six months or a year. Comments and criticisms from the staff using the standards can be gathered and analyzed. The standards then can be revised upwards or downwards as needed to correct any problems encountered during the trial period. A year or more may be needed to fine-tune performance standards.

## EDUCATION AND TRAINING OF STAFF

An education and training program for the staff of the automated library function is vital. If staff do not understand how to perform their assigned jobs or the basic principles underlying automation, the general capabilities and limitations of the computer supporting the function, and how to work and interact with the computer in their daily activities, then the automated function has little chance to succeed. The more staff know about their jobs and how their work fits into the overall picture, the better they can perform their jobs and, consequently, the better the automated function will be.

In educating and training staff to work in the automated function, several steps might be taken.

### Orienting Staff to Automation in General

All staff who will work in the automated library function should be given an orientation to automation in general. Everyone, regardless of responsibilities within the function, should have a basic understanding of computers and automation. This basic education could enable staff to gain better insight into their jobs, give better service to users, and become more valuable employees in general.

There are several alternatives for educating staff about automation in general. One way is through formal courses offered by the library's host institution, a nearby college or university, or other educational institutions or groups. For most staff, the course should be on a survey or introductory level. The library should allow staff time with pay to attend such courses and should, if possible, pay tuition and other expenses related to the course.

Another typical method of educating staff for automation is through workshops and seminars sponsored by the library or by others, held in the library or at other locations. Many local, state, regional, and national library organizations sponsor such educational opportunities year-round in various parts of the country and at nominal costs. Many are held during library conferences. The library should allow staff time with pay to attend such sessions and should, if possible, pay expenses such as travel, per diem, and registration for attending.

Staff can learn much about computers and automation through self-paced instruction. A reading list or text is supplied to the staff member, who reads the material at his or her own pace. If available, Computer Assisted Instruction (CAI) courses can be used effectively for teaching staff about automation. The library should prepare the reading list, provide staff with the material or CAI system, and allow staff time to read the material or use the CAI system.

Touring other libraries with automated functions is another way of educating library staff about automation. Staff can see and examine automated functions and talk with staff who manage and operate them. If there are no automated functions in nearby libraries, special trips can be organized, or staff can be encouraged to visit automated libraries when attending conferences in other cities. The library should allow staff time with pay for site visits and pay expenses for the visits when possible.

Staff can learn about computers and automation by visiting exhibits at library and other related conferences and meetings. Staff can usually see and operate equipment, listen to presentations by vendor representatives, see demonstrations of the equipment, and ask questions when information is not clear. The library should allow staff time with pay to attend conferences with exhibits and pay expenses when possible.

One of the best methods of educating staff about computers and automation is to involve them extensively in the automation project. As they serve on advisory committees or assist in other ways, staff can be introduced to the new topics. Usually, staff are willing and eager to learn when they see an obvious need for new knowledge.

## Orienting Staff to the Automated Function in General

Staff should be oriented in general to the automated library function in which they will work. This orientation can be provided by the vendor who sold the automated system to the library, by the library's automation librarian, or by the manager of the automated function.

Orientation to the automated function should include as a minimum:

1. A general overview of the automated function.
2. How the automated function fits into the total automation program of the library.
3. A general description and demonstration of each of the function's components and their features.
4. A tour and demonstration of the computer system supporting the automated function.

## Training Staff to Operate Equipment

Staff should be trained to operate the computer terminals and other special equipment essential to their work. As a minimum, the staff should be able to:

1. Understand the basic purpose and operation of the equipment in the automated function.
2. Identify each part of equipment and its specific function.
3. Turn on, turn off, adjust, check, and clean the equipment.
4. Operate the equipment.
5. Identify problems with the equipment and take necessary action to prevent damage to the equipment until supervisory staff arrive.

## Providing Specific Job Training

Each staff member should be instructed how to perform his or her new duties and responsibilities in the automated function. The immediate supervisor of each person should provide the training. The following guidelines for job training are offered:

1. Give the employee a copy of the new procedure manual for the automated function.
2. Gather all materials, supplies, etc., which will be used in the training.
3. Arrange the workstation just as the employee will be expected to keep it.
4. Place the employee at ease.
5. Present the new duties slowly to the employee by describing, illustrating, and performing the tasks, one point at a time.
6. Ask if the employee understands the tasks and repeat the instructions if necessary.
7. Let the employee perform the tasks.
8. Observe the performance, correct any errors, and repeat the instructions if necessary.
9. Let the employee practice on his or her own.
10. Check frequently to see how the employee is progressing.
11. Continue observing the employee, but check less frequently as he or she builds up speed and confidence.

Training should be conducted in the workplace where the employee will be performing his or her new duties and on the same or similar equipment that he or she will use on a daily basis.

## Providing Follow-Up Training

Follow-up training should be provided to reinforce what the staff have learned, to allow identification and correction of problems encountered during the first sessions, and to enable the staff to ask additional questions after they have more confidence and have overcome the initial trauma of learning something new.

## Providing Continuing Education

The need for a continual education of staff of the automated library function should be recognized and provided for. A continuing education program for all staff is needed to keep them current with the changes taking place in the workplace and in automation in general and to teach staff new skills as needed.

Continuing education opportunities can be offered in-house by library staff or by outside specialists, or staff can be sent to courses, seminars, and the like in the library's host institution, elsewhere in the community, or at distant points where learning opportunities are offered.

## ADDITIONAL READINGS

Berenson, Conrad, and Henry O. Ruhnke. *Job Descriptions: How to Write and Use Them*. Santa Monica, CA: Personnel Journal, 1974.

Corbin, John. "Staff and User Education and Training." In *Managing the Library Automation Project*. Phoenix: Oryx Press, 1985: 158-68.

Cowley, John. *Personnel Management in Libraries*. London: Bingley, 1982.

Creth, Sheila. *Effective On-the-Job Training: Developing Library Human Resources*. Chicago: American Library Association, 1986.

———. "Personnel Planning, Job Analysis, and Job Evaluation with Special Reference to Academic Libraries." In *Advances in Librarianship*. Vol. 12, edited by Wesley Simonton. New York: Academic Press, 1982: 47-72.

Dagnese, Joseph M. "Managing Organizational Change: MRAP As a Vehicle." In *Emerging Trends in Library Organization: What Influences Change*, edited by Sul H. Lee. Ann Arbor, MI: Pierian Press, 1978: 13-25.

Davis, Louis E., and James C. Taylor, comps. *Design of Jobs*. 2nd ed. Santa Monica, CA: Goodyear Publishing Company, 1979.

Drabenstott, Jon. "Automation Planning and Organizational Change: A Functional Model for Developing a Systems Plan." *Library Hi Tech* 3 (No.3, 1986): 15-24.

Ferguson, Anthony W., and John R. Taylor. "'What Are You Doing?' An Analysis of Activities of Public Service Librarians at a Medium-Sized Research Library." *Journal of Academic Librarianship* 6 (March 1980): 24-29.

Fine, Sidney A. and Wretha W. Wiley. *An Introduction to Functional Job Analysis.* (Methods for Manpower Analysis, No. 4). W.E. Upjohn Institute for Employment Research, 1971.

FitzGerald, Patricia A., Patricia Arnott, and Deborah Richards. "Computer-Assisted Instruction in Libraries: Guidelines for Effective Lesson Design." *Library Hi Tech* 4 (Summer 1986): 29-37.

Gael, Sidney. *Job Analysis: A Guide to Assessing Work Activities.* San Francisco, CA: Jossey-Bass, 1983.

Hill, V.S., and T.G. Watson. "Job Analysis: Process and Benefits." In *Advances in Library Administration and Organization.* Vol.3. Greenwich, CT: JAI Press, 1984: 209-19.

Horny, Karen L. "Managing Change: Technology & the Profession." *Library Journal* 110 (October 1, 1985): 56-58.

Jones, Noragh, and Peter J. Jordan. *Staff Management in Library and Information Work.* London: Gower, 1982.

Little, Thompson M. "Technological Advances and Organizational Change." In *Emerging Trends in Library Organization: What Influences Change,* edited by Sul H. Lee. Ann Arbor, MI: Pierian Press, 1978: 39-48.

McCormick, Ernest J. "Job and Task Analysis." In *Handbook of Industrial Engineering,* edited by Gavriel Salvendy. New York: Wiley, 1982: 2.4.1-21.

Marchionini, Gary, and Danuta A. Nitecki. "Managing Change: Supporting Users of Automated Systems." *College & Research Libraries* 48 (March 1987): 104-09.

Miller, Mary Jane. "Constructing Job Descriptions for Library Support Staff Positions: A Modular Approach." In *Managing the Electronic Library. Papers of the 1982 Conference of the Library Management Division of Special Libraries Association,* edited by Michael Koenig. New York: Special Libraries Association, 1983: 32-45.

Mugnier, Charlotte. *The Paraprofessional and the Professional Job Structure.* Chicago: American Library Association, 1980.

Panico, Joseph A. "Work Standards: Establishment, Documentation, Usage, and Maintenance." In *Handbook of Industrial Engineering,* edited by Gavriel Salvendy. New York: Wiley, 1982: 4.1.1-25.

*Personnel Administration in Libraries,* edited by Sheila Creth and Frederick Duda. New York: Neal-Schuman, 1981.

Ricking, Myrl, and Robert E. Booth. *Personnel Utilization in Libraries: A Systems Approach.* Chicago: American Library Association, 1974.

Stone, Elizabeth. "The Growth of Continuing Education." *Library Trends* 34 (Winter 1986): 489-513.

Stueart, Robert D. "Preparing Libraries for Change." *Library Journal* 109 (September 15, 1984): 1724-26.

Tenopir, Carol. "In-House Training & Staff Development." *Library Journal* 109 (May 1, 1984): 870-71.

Yglesias, Donna B. "Improving Staff Creativity, Productivity and Accountability." In *Austerity Management in Academic Libraries,* edited by John F. Harvey and Peter Spyers-Duran. Metuchen, NJ: Scarecrow Press, 1984: 255-68.

# Chapter 6
# Space Planning and Design

The planning and design of the physical space in which an automated library function will be housed is the subject of this chapter. The purpose of space planning and design is to optimize the effectiveness and efficiency of the function being automated through the careful arrangement of its floorspace and the planning of its environment.

The process is more than just arranging furniture and equipment for an automated function in a floorspace layout. It is viewing the physical space itself as a system in which the functions to be performed, the required workstations, the needs of the individual who will work in the system, essential supervision and communication, storage, furniture and equipment, lighting, color, noise control, and physical and environmental factors all interrelate and interact.

The introduction of an automated function into existing space may require as little as a minor shifting of furniture and the installation of computer cables, or as much as extensive renovation of quarters and the purchase of new furniture and equipment. The manager of the automated function should, if possible, take advantage of the event by streamlining the workspace and eliminating old and unnecessary furniture.

The purpose of this chapter is to discuss the planning and design of space for an automated library function. Its topics include:

- The space planning and design team
- The space planning and design plan
- Space planning and design consultants
- Space planning and design concept options
- The choice of space planning and design concept
- Square footage requirements
- Adjacency requirements
- Power and signal distribution
- The floorspace layout
- Environmental design
- Space planning and design specifications
- Implementation costs
- The space planning and design report

## THE SPACE PLANNING AND DESIGN TEAM

The first step in planning and designing the space for an automated library function is to assemble a team to be responsible for the effort. The formation of such a group can provide an excellent means of involving staff in implementing the automated function. Of concern will be the team's responsibilities and membership.

### Responsibilities of the Team

The space planning and design team should be given a clear, unambiguous charge or set of responsibilities. The specific responsibilities assigned to the team will depend upon the nature of the automated function, the extent to which the space of an existing function can or should be reorganized or renovated, and the funds available to the library for the implementation of the design.

*Example*: The space planning and design team shall: (1) develop a set of space requirements of the automated function; (2) develop a recommended floorspace layout for the automated function's activities; (3) prepare specifications for purchasing the furniture and equipment recommended; (4) estimate costs of implementing the plan recommended; and (5) prepare a report of the planning and design project.

### Members of the Team

Once the responsibilities of the space planning and design team have been clearly delineated, its members can be selected and appointed. The team, which should be composed of key staff of the function being automated, might have from three to seven members, depending upon the size of the library's staff, the extent of the planning and design to be done, and the time allotted for its completion. Those to serve on the team should be chosen for their expertise or for their potential for contributing to the successful completion of the project. A chair of the team may be appointed, or the members may elect their own leader.

## THE SPACE PLANNING AND DESIGN PROJECT PLAN

The space planning and design process for an automated library function should be considered a project unto itself and should be well planned. The plan need not be elaborate or lengthy, but should, as a minimum, include planning and design goals, planning and design constraints, planning and design activities, a planning and design schedule, and a planning and design budget.

## Planning and Design Goals

The team should clearly define its goals for planning and designing the space for the automated function. The goals will provide guidelines to follow when studying space requirements and developing the floorspace layout and other specifications.

*Example*: Planning and design goals should strive to plan and design space for the automated function that: (1) is flexible; (2) optimizes the effectiveness and efficiency of the function; (4) enhances the comfort, productivity, and motivation of library staff and users; and (5) is aesthetically pleasing.

The planning and design goals should be documented, discussed, and approved by both the team and key managers of the automated function before work is begun.

## Planning and Design Constraints

Any constraints to be placed on the space planning and design effort by library management, the manager of the automated function, or others should be identified. These constraints will limit or place conditions on the undertaking.

*Example*: Space planning and design constraints state that: (1) a planning and design report must be ready in 60 days; (2) existing furniture must be utilized in the new design; (3) the space for the automated function must be reduced by 25% from the existing function; and (4) the cost of implementing the design must not exceed $—.

The constraints also should be documented, discussed, and approved by the planning and design team and others before work is begun. The planning and design goals and the constraints can be discussed and approved at the same time.

## Planning and Design Activities

The space planning and design team should establish a strategy for fulfilling its charge. The strategy can be in the form of an outline of the activities expected to be accomplished in order to complete the planning and design work successfully, just as was developed for the automation project as a whole as described in Chapter 2. This plan also should be dynamic; that is, the activities should be altered as work progresses and as new conditions and situations arise. For example, if after an analysis of requirements of the automated function for space, the team discovers that existing furniture is inadequate, then plans might be changed to develop specifications for new purchases.

## The Planning and Design Schedule

After the outline of work to be done has been developed, discussed, and approved, a schedule or calendar for completing the activities should be prepared. Either a Gantt chart or a network chart, discussed in Chapter 2, can be used.

## The Planning and Design Budget

An estimate of the funds needed to complete the space planning and design project can be prepared by the team and submitted to the appropriate budget authorities for approval before work begins.

The budget should include those expenses necessary to study and plan the requirements of the automated system for space, prepare the floorspace layout, develop other specifications, and prepare the final project report. Funds also may be required during the project to secure the services of specialists or consultants who will assist the team in preparing the layout and other specifications. Funds for implementing the recommendations of the team should not be included in this budget. These costs will be estimated by the team in the course of its work and included as a part of its final report.

## SPACE PLANNING AND DESIGN CONSULTANTS

Some aspects of space planning and design will require specialized and highly technical knowledge. One or more consultants or a consulting firm may be utilized to ensure effective results of its efforts. For example, interior designers, electrical contractors, and lighting specialists may be used for their particular knowledge and talents. Manufacturer representatives and vendors can also contribute to the planning and design project. In some cases, the team may feel that a consultant would be more objective than library staff in analyzing a situation and in reaching conclusions regarding a design.

Of concern should be determining the consultant services required, locating consultants, and securing consultants' services.

### Determining the Consultant Services Required

The specific services required of a consultant by the space planning and design team will depend upon how extensive and technical its work will be. Typical services a consultant might offer could be to educate the members on topics such as space planning in general, color, lighting, or furniture; recommend specifications for color schemes, lighting, floor treatments, or electrical requirements; prepare technical specifications for furniture, equipment, electrical installations, color schemes, or lighting; and assist in locating vendors and in purchasing goods and services required to implement the design.

A statement detailing specifically the work to be performed should be prepared before selection of a consultant is begun.

*Example*: The consultant is to examine the space for the automated function and the plans of the planning and design team and recommend specific lighting fixtures and their locations for enhancing working conditions in the space.

*Example*: The consultant is to work with the planning and design team to: (1) determine the electrical load requirements of the automated function; (2) identify the location of electrical outlets in the space; and (3) prepare specifications for the purchase of materials for implementing the recommendations.

## Locating Consultants

In many cases, the library will have specialists within its parent organization or institution who can serve as consultants to the library during a space planning and design project. For example, specialists may be on the facilities and planning staff on an academic library's campus, in a public library's city government, or in a special library's corporation. The services of these people may be available to the library upon request, perhaps at nominal or no cost.

If the expertise required for the project is not available within the library's parent organization or institution, the library may have to hire an outside consultant or consulting firm. In this case, consultants can be identified by seeking recommendations from the library's purchasing or planning department or from colleagues and friends. Potential consultants then can be interviewed to determine which have the best skills and resources to meet the team's needs.

## Securing Consultants' Services

Services of a consultant may be secured either informally or formally. If the consultant is from the staff of the library's parent organization or institution, no written agreement or formal contract may be required for his or her services. However, a written request for use of the specialist's time may be required for accountability purposes. To obtain the services of an outside consultant, the library may be required to follow bidding procedures and the awarding of a contract based upon the best and lowest bid.

## SPACE PLANNING AND DESIGN CONCEPT OPTIONS

The space planning and design team may wish to study several space planning concepts as a prelude to studying and analyzing the space needs of the automated library function. The three most common concepts are the closed concept, the open concept, and the mixed concept.

### The Closed Concept

In the closed concept of space planning, fixed walls enclose offices, workrooms, conference rooms, and reception areas assigned to individuals or to groups of staff. Supervisory staff usually are assigned the most desirable offices, usually defined by size, attractiveness, and number of outside windows.

The closed concept of space planning has a number of advantages. Maximum privacy for individuals and groups of staff can be provided, security can be provided to enclosed areas by locking doors, sound can be controlled by isolating noisy operations in enclosed areas, and the heating, cooling, and ventilation of enclosed areas can be controlled individually. Disadvantages to the concept include future inflexibility of space caused by the walls of the enclosed areas, restricted interaction of individuals and groups, and the need for more floor space over other concepts due to the necessity of walls and doors.

### The Open Concept

In contrast to the closed concept, the open concept of space planning is characterized by the lack of fixed walls. There are several common variations of the open concept.

One variation is the "bullpen" arrangement, in which workstations and other furniture and equipment are placed in a grid pattern with straight aisles between the rows. Few or no partitions are used to separate areas. This concept has been used in business offices for many years, and some technical services areas in libraries use such a layout for their quarters. However, to the staff who must work in the "bullpen," the arrangement implies regimentation, noise, and a subsequent lack of concern for the individual. The only time this type of open arrangement works well is when the number of workstations is limited and the open space where the workstations are placed is small and perhaps irregularly shaped. In this case, the intimacy of the workspace can reduce the feeling of regimentation.

A more acceptable variation of the open concept is the placement of staff in an area without floor-to-ceiling walls, but with workstations encircled by movable partitions of varying heights to screen staff from each other. Even conference areas are unenclosed except by head-high partitions. This approach softens the regimented look of "bullpen" workspace.

A unique variation of the open concept is office landscaping, which stresses an irregular placement of workstations and the use of many plants to further break the feeling of regimentation. This concept is characterized by a careful and systematic planning of all elements of the space, such as communications, relationships of workstations to each other, lighting, etc.

The open concept, then, has some distinct advantages. It connotes efficiency, clean lines, and orderliness; interaction of individuals and groups is maximized; supervisors can have clear views of their areas of responsibilities; and the arrangement is simple and flexible, in that changes can be made easily by moving partitions and the modular furniture. Even electrical, telephone, and computer cables embedded in the floor or in the ceiling can be reorganized to meet changing space needs when required. Disadvantages include the lack of privacy, noise, and no individual control of air conditioning and heating as in enclosed offices.

### The Mixed Concept

The most typical approach to the planning and design of space for a system is the mixed concept, where the best features of the closed and the open plans are combined. Usually, areas with floor-to-ceiling walls are provided only for supervisory staff, conference rooms, and other functions that must be isolated due to their generation of noise. Other areas are open, perhaps arranged in a combination of ways. For example, some workstations may be arranged in "bullpen" fashion, others by simple movable partitions, and others by office landscaping. This approach lends itself to the variety of functions, responsibilities, and processing modes commonly found in automated systems.

### THE CHOICE OF SPACE PLANNING AND DESIGN CONCEPT

After the options for space planning and design have been studied and discussed, one concept must be selected for the automated function. The final decision as to which concept to follow need not be made until the space planning and design team is ready to prepare the floorspace layout, but a tentative choice can be made at any time. The advantages and disadvantages of each planning and design concept must be weighed and other factors considered as the decision is being made.

The space planning and design concept ultimately chosen for the automated library function will depend upon such factors as the location of the automated function, compatibility with other space in the building, the configuration of the space for the function, and the funds available to the library.

## The Location of the Automated Function

The location of the automated function within the library will influence its floorspace arrangement. For example, if an automated circulation function is being installed in a public area of the library, there may be a need to retain a sense of openness, so that the staff can retain eyesight supervision over large areas. Therefore, the open concept of space planning may be essential. However, if a nonpublic function such as acquisitions or bibliographic control is being installed, the need for openness is diminished, and either the closed, the open, or the mixed concept could be used.

## Compatibility with Other Space in the Building

Architects, interior designers, and library management usually attempt to maintain a compatible style of furniture and equipment throughout a building, particularly in public areas. Therefore, the choice of a space planning and design concept for the automated function will be influenced by the compatibility of the proposed arrangement and furnishings with those of other functions.

For example, office landscaping placed alongside the decidedly traditional furniture in adjacent space may look out of place, unless an eclectic look is being sought. On the other hand, moving from an area of the library with one style of furnishings and decoration to another area with a totally different look can be exciting, if the furnishings are selected and arranged well.

## The Configuration of the Space for the Function

The configuration of the space allotted the automated function will influence the decision as to which planning and design concept to use. For example, if the space where the function will be located is already divided into enclosed areas by load-bearing walls, the closed concept of space layout may be chosen, unless extensive renovation can be undertaken. However, if the space is simply a large open area, a variation of the open concept may be chosen.

## The Funds Available to the Library

The funds available to the library to implement a particular space planning concept will influence its choice of floorspace arrangement for an automated function. Office landscaping, for example, may be rejected as an option, due to the high cost of the modular furniture and the partitions required in relation to more traditional furniture.

## SQUARE FOOTAGE REQUIREMENTS

The amount of floorspace required for the automated library function should be defined. Since there are no universally-recognized standards for space requirements in libraries, the space planning and design team will have to gather typical figures from several sources and adopt those that appear to be most applicable to the space for the automated system being implemented.

Of concern are square footage requirements of workstations, floorspace for trafficways, and floorspace for other furniture and equipment. Defining these requirements will provide a means for determining the total square feet of space to house the automated function.

### Square Footage Requirements of Workstations

Since a workstation is designed to suit the specific activities and operations assigned to the staff using it, the square footage may vary from workstation to workstation, depending upon the furniture and equipment required.

The floorspace to be allotted to a workstation with or without a computer terminal includes space for a desk or table, a chair, other furniture and equipment, and circulation within the workstation. For example, to calculate the square feet of floorspace needed for a workstation, the furniture, such as a desk or table and a chair, is laid out on grid paper. These might require 27½ square feet. Space for circulation around the workstation might add two feet on all sides of the station. Thus, 85½ total square feet of floor space are required for the workstation.

Clustered workstations will require less floorspace because a circulation area between and behind each station is not required. For example, four workstations clustered together would require 210 square feet of floorspace, as opposed to 342 square feet if they were separated. A further discussion of workstations can be found in Chapter 7.

### Floorspace for Trafficways

A part of the space for an automated function must be allotted for traffic into, out of, and through the area. While an aisle width of three feet would be a minimum, additional space should be allowed, if possible, to avoid crowding. For example, if abundant space is available for the automated function, a trafficway of six feet may be generous, but with space at a premium, the aisle may have to be reduced to four feet.

### Floorspace for Other Furniture and Equipment

Floorspace standards for other furniture and equipment, such as filing cabinets, shelving, office credenzas, printers, etc., can be calculated by laying out the item to scale on grid paper, adding circulation space in front of or around it, and multiplying the length by the width of the layout. For example, 78 square feet of floorspace will be required for a bay of freestanding, double-sided shelving of three sections long, with two feet of circulation space on all sides.

## ADJACENCY REQUIREMENTS

The physical placement of activities and of workstations and other furniture and equipment in relation to each other in the floorspace should be studied.

Relationships between staff in units of the automated library function must be considered for library users to staff, group to group interaction, and group to ancillary activities such as function managers, a conference room, supplies storage, and the computer supporting the automated function. Relationships of workstations and other furniture and equipment within a group of staff must be considered for library user to staff, staff members to equipment, staff members to storage areas, staff members to supervisors, and staff members to other staff.

There are several tools or techniques that can be used in studying adjacency requirements in an automated library function. These include bubble diagrams, the zone formation diagram, and the flow diagram.

### Bubble Diagrams

The bubble diagram, illustrated in Figure 6-1, is one of the best tools for studying adjacency requirements of the automated function.

The intragroup bubble diagram can be used to study the needs for adjacency of the activities of the function. Circles of varying sizes are drawn to represent the activities of the function. The size of a circle can indicate the relative differences in size of the activity. Lines are drawn between the circles to indicate needs for adjacency. The circles can be moved until optimum adjacency between all the activities is achieved.

The personal bubble diagram can be used to study the relationships between library users, staff, and ancillary activities *within* a function. Circles are drawn to represent staff, users, and ancillary

**FIGURE 6-1. The Bubble Diagram**

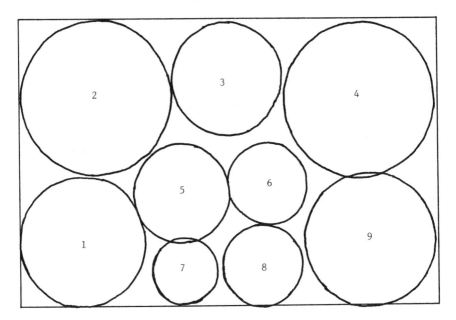

```
1 = TERMINAL A
2 = TERMINAL B
3 = TERMINAL C
4 = TERMINAL D
5 = CLERK-TYPIST
6 = DOCUMENTATION
7 = SUPPLIES
8 = RECEPTIONIST
9 = TERMINAL E
```

activities. Lines are drawn between the circles to indicate a need for adjacency of workstations or closeness to ancillary areas. As the diagram is analyzed, the circles are moved until staff and users are closest to those others with whom they must most interact.

Often, there will be a need to locate an automated function close to other functions, automated or manual. The intergroup bubble diagram can be used to study the relationships between functions in the library. Circles are drawn to represent the functions, and lines are drawn between them to indicate a need for adjacency. The circles can be moved about until the best adjacency is obtained for all functions. The greatest use for the intergroup bubble diagram will be during a new building program or when extensive renovation to an existing building will be undertaken before the automated function is implemented.

## The Zone Formation Diagram

The preparation of a zone formation diagram can assist the space planning and design team in visualizing the activities that should occupy prime and nonprime space and in ensuring good planning of traffic and circulation through the areas when the automated function will be installed.

Zone formation is the depiction of the arrangement of groups of people in the space to be allotted to functional and ancillary activities and major trafficways. It is the superimposition of the bubble diagram, discussed above, onto the representation of the workspace in order to determine how the activities of the automated function will fit into the space.

To construct the diagram, physical areas or zones for basic and ancillary activities are laid out to scale on the floor plan (Figure 6-2). The zones should not overlap. No workstations or other furniture and equipment are indicated at this time. Major traffic corridors are drawn, also to scale. The traffic ways should not be perpendicular or parallel to each other and should be located between, rather than through, functional groupings of staff. The shape of the zones can be adjusted for the best spatial relationships between activities and to provide good circulation and traffic patterns.

## The Flow Diagram

The flow diagram can be useful in studying the flow of work and materials through the floorspace for the automated function. A sketch of the floorspace is made, not necessarily to scale, with locations of workstations and other furniture and equipment shown (Figure 6-3). The movement of people and materials is traced from workstation to workstation as operations will be performed. The paths are shown as lines drawn on the sketch, with the direction of movement shown by arrowheads on the lines. The movement of multiple people or materials can be shown by lines of different colors.

Excessive bottlenecks of staff or materials, circulation traffic routes, or long distances for specific staff and materials to travel can indicate a need to relocate workstations and other furniture and equipment until these problems are minimized.

**FIGURE 6-2. The Zone Formation Diagram**

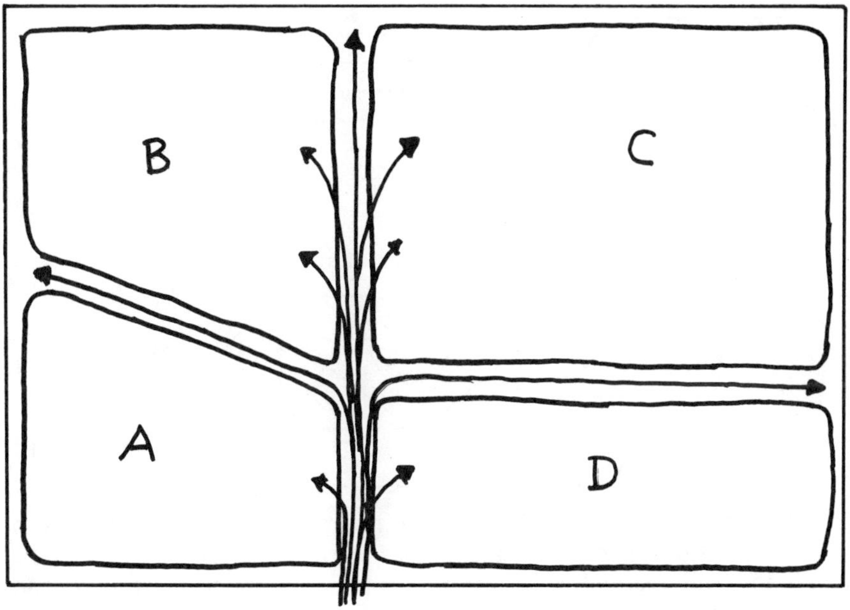

```
A =   STORAGE FOR MATERIALS, TOOLS, DOCUMENTATION
B =   DATA ENTRY
C =   CATALOGING STAFF
D =   MANAGEMENT STAFF, RECEPTION, CONFERENCE
```

## POWER AND SIGNAL DISTRIBUTION

Requirements of the automated library function for power and signal distribution should be prepared. The space planning and design team should study the needs of the function for power and its distribution, telephones and their locations, and computer cables and their locations.

### Power and Its Distribution

The electrical power requirements and physical location of each piece of equipment, including computer terminals, to be used in the automated function should be determined. An electrician can be consulted to determine the need of each piece of equipment for energy, the type of receptacle to install, the total power load required by the automated function, and ways the energy can be distributed correctly and efficiently.

**FIGURE 6-3. The Flow Diagram**

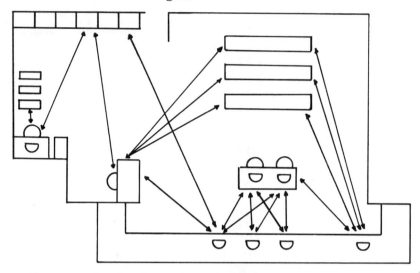

Power can be distributed from the floor, the ceiling, or the walls to the workstations and other locations where electrical energy will be required. The method used for the automated function will depend upon pre-existing construction and the funds available to the library. Wall connections for power distribution are common, but they can restrict the placement of workstations and other equipment close to the walls. Also, wires from wall receptacles to workstations in the center of the room can be unsightly and potential traffic and fire hazards. Electrical wiring can be channeled from the ceiling to workstations via vertical power poles that are usually unnoticeable in an open area, particularly when half-height partitions are used. They can be easily and inexpensively moved to new locations when changes in the workspace become necessary. Floor connections are the best solution for bringing electrical power to workstations, although possibly slightly more expensive than other methods. The outlet boxes can sit on the floor or be flush with it. This method enables cables to be brought directly to workstations without use of power poles or potentially dangerous cable bridges.

## Telephones and Their Locations

The number and location of telephone instruments in the floorspace for the automated function should be determined. A communications specialist can assist the space planning and design team in ascertaining the types of telephone instruments to install, the number of lines needed, and other special communications needs. Telephone cables can be placed in the same conduits as electric wiring.

## Computer Cables and Their Locations

After the exact location of each computer terminal has been de-cided, the space planning and design team should consult the library's automation or systems librarian about connecting the devices to the computer supporting the automated function. The automation librar-ian, in conjunction with the vendor of the automated system being installed, can assist in determining how the terminals will be connected and where the computer cables, if any, should be installed and the size and type to use. Computer cables can be placed in the same or in separate conduits as electric wiring and telephone cables.

## COMPUTER HARDWARE CONNECTIONS

Workstations will be located at the points in the library where services or processing needing access to a computer are offered or performed. This may be several hundred feet, blocks, or miles away from the computer supporting the automated library function. How-ever, the devices in the workstation must be connected to the computer in some manner. The common means of accomplishing this are using direct cable connections, leased telephone line connections, dial-up telephone line connections, and local area network connections.

## Direct Cable Connections

The most reliable method of connecting devices in a workstation to a computer system is directly by cable (Figure 6-4). One end of the cable is plugged into the back of the terminal, and the other end into an interface port at the back of the computer.

Coaxial cable is commonly used to link a terminal to a computer when the distance between the two is less than several hundred feet. The exact distance will depend upon the cable used and the conditions under which it is laid. Using cable is ineffective for distances over several hundred feet because signal distortion makes the connection undesirable. For distances over several hundred feet, twisted-pair wire can be used up to a mile or so if limited-distance or short-haul modems are used. One modem is placed at the computer end and another at the workstation end (Figure 6-5). Usually, it is impractical and uneconomical for the library to install cabling of any type for distances of more than a 1,000 feet. Where the distance is greater, use of leased lines or a dial-up arrangement provides a better alternative.

**FIGURE 6-4. Direct Cable Connections of Terminals to a Computer System**

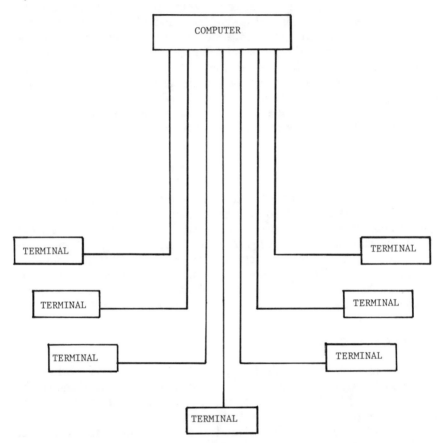

## Leased Telephone Line Connections

A private or leased telephone line can be used to connect a terminal located further than several hundred feet from its computer. The leased line is a permanent transmission link provided between the terminal and its computer and reserved for the sole, unlimited use of the library. The line is provided by a public communications common carrier utility such as AT&T, General Telephone, and others. The line remains connected for the duration of a contract or lease between the library and the utility. Special equipment can be added to the leased line by the utility to minimize "noise" on the link and, consequently, provide a high quality of transmission.

A modem must be used to convert the digital signal generated by the terminal into a form suitable for transmission over the telephone line. Another modem at the computer restores the data back to its

**FIGURE 6-5. Terminals Connected to a Computer System Using Modems**

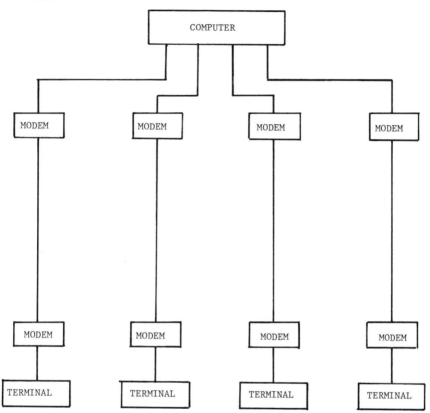

original digital form. A variety of modems is available for use with leased lines, priced according to speed of transmission and other features; the higher the speed, the higher the price of the device. For terminals used heavily by staff or the public, where speed of transmission to and from the computer is important, high-speed modems are a necessity. Most minicomputer and mainframe computers supporting library applications can readily support speeds up to 9600 Baud.

Some other communications devices may be used to increase the efficiency of terminal use and decrease the costs of telecommunications for the library. A multiplexer is a device that enables a number of low-speed or low-activity terminals to have economic access to a computer by sharing the same leased line. The device combines the signals from the several workstations and transmits them simultaneously over one common line. A multiplexer at the other end of the line separates the signals before information is sent to the computer for processing. Modems are still required with this arrangement (Figure

6-6). Other devices, such as concentrators and front-end processors, are used at the computer site only to improve telecommunications for an automated library function.

**FIGURE 6-6. Multiplexed Terminals**

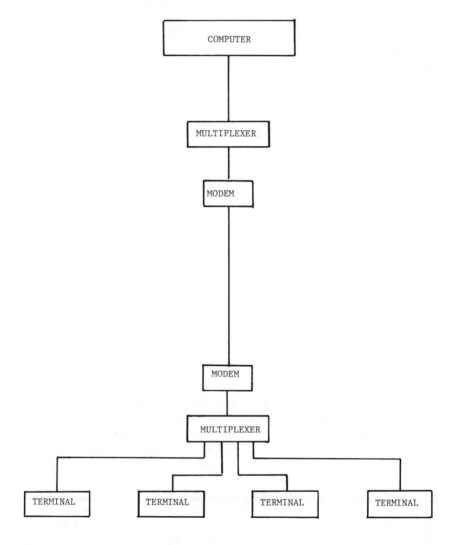

## Dial-Up Telephone Line Connections

A third method of connecting a terminal to the computer support-ing an automated library function is through a dial-up telephone arrangement. This approach might be used for low-usage terminals or when a microcomputer is used as a terminal.

The dial-up arrangement is similar to the leased line connection described above, except that the connection is made through an operator or an automatic switching center of some type. A modem and a telephone instrument with either touch-tone or rotary dial capabilities is essential for a dial-up connection. The number of the computer is dialed. When the high-pitched computer tone is heard, a hook is pulled or a button pushed on the instrument to make the connection. For some terminals, including microcomputer terminals, communications software can make the connection to the remote computer, so no telephone instrument is required. Either a stand-alone modem or a modem on a circuit board inside the terminal may be used. The dial-up link is available to the library as long as a connection is made, and the cost is determined by the mileage between the terminal and its computer, the time of the day or night, and the duration of the connect time.

A benefit of using a dial-up arrangement is that a terminal can be located inexpensively anywhere in the library where a telephone line can be installed. A disadvantage is that dial-up lines are subject to high error rates due to "noise" on the line. Also, dialing up the computer each time the terminal is to be used will be bothersome. If a terminal must be used by the staff or the public for long periods of time throughout each day, a leased line connection will be more practical.

## Local Area Network Connections

A local area network or LAN may be used to connect a terminal to the computer system supporting an automated library function. A local area network is a data communications network located within a building, a campus, or other limited geographic area and meant to serve only the library or the library and its parent institution or organization. The LAN can be used to replace the cables between the computer and its terminals.

An advantage to using a local area network to connect terminals to a computer is that interface with, or access to, different automated systems from the same terminal may be easier. Thus, the movement of information from one automated system to another could be facilitated.

## THE FLOORSPACE LAYOUT

After all requirements of the automated function for space have been identified, analyzed, and synthesized, the floorspace layout can be prepared. The layout will indicate the positioning of workstations and other furniture and equipment within the physical space for the function.

Of use will be a scaled representation of the space, preliminary layouts, and the final layout.

## A Scaled Representation of the Space

A scaled representation of the space where the automated function will be located should be prepared. The floorspace layout will be prepared using this representation, which can be a copy of the architectural or construction blueprints of the space or a sketch drawn to scale on grid or blank paper. Computer graphics or Computer Assisted Design (CAD) software could provide a pictorial simulation model of the workspace which can be used in floorspace layout. The boundaries of the space and the location of pillars or columns, windows, partitions, and doors should be shown on the representation.

## Preliminary Layouts

Several alternative layouts of the most likely arrangements for the workspace can be prepared. The alternatives then can be discussed and rated by staff and management and the most suitable one chosen for the final layout. A preliminary sketch showing workstations as circles of varying sizes within each zone formation also may be useful.

## The Final Layout

After any preliminary layouts have been prepared and discussed and the best approved, the final layout can be prepared. Workstations and other furniture and equipment should be laid out on the representation of the space, one group at a time, using the square footages adopted as space standards.

There are several techniques for preparing the layout, including pasting cutouts of workstations and other furniture and equipment on the floorspace representation, using a template to draw scaled workstations and other furniture and equipment on the representation, and using computer software to prepare pictorial simulations of the workstation and other furniture and equipment, if computer graphics or Computer Assisted Design is used.

As the final layout emerges, the team should keep several rules of thumb in mind:

> 1. Workstations and other furniture and equipment within a grouping should be parallel in order to maximize the staff's

feeling of spaciousness. Staff do not all have to face in the same direction, however.
2. Good circulation or traffic within each grouping should be maintained.
3. Space for a group should not be approachable from the rear.
4. Access to one workstation should never interfere with other workstations.
5. Staff should face toward the entry into a group space.
6. Circulation or traffic routes should be as direct and short as possible.

## ENVIRONMENTAL DESIGN

The floorspace layout will indicate for the automated library function specifically where its workstations, other furniture and equipment, telephones, circulation space, and trafficways will be located. Of further concern are lighting, color and graphics, and noise control.

### Lighting

The requirements of the automated library function for lighting of its space should be prepared. A lighting specialist should be consulted during this step. The lighting should provide equally pleasant, glare-free working conditions for all workstations in the function. For library staff, good lighting can result in improved productivity, a higher quality of work, better security, and improved staff morale. For library users, good lighting provides adequate illumination to perform basic tasks and reduces eyestrain and mental fatigue.

Several considerations should be made for lighting for the automated function, including the specific tasks to be performed, the brightness of the lighting source, the composition of the workspace, building and safety codes, maintenance of the lighting and installation, and energy costs.

### Color and Graphics

The colors used in the space for an automated function should be carefully chosen to enhance staff productivity and mental and physical health by making the workspace pleasant. Graphics should be integrated into the color scheme, not only to inform staff and users, but to be decorative.

People are strongly affected by the colors around them. Shades of blue tend to be restful by lowering blood pressure and pulse rates, while reds have the opposite effect. Greens and grays are neutral. Most find that autumn colors are the best over long periods of time. The size and shape of the room, the number of windows, how the space will be used, and the furniture and equipment to be in the space will also affect the choice of color scheme. Since light and color are interrelated, the team should consider the two together. Specific colors for the walls, ceilings, and floor covering of the workspace must be chosen within the overall color scheme. The color and finish of furniture and equipment should be chosen to be in harmony with the colors selected for the walls, ceiling, and floor covering. Graphics are useful to identify the functions within a workspace, to give directions, or to provide other useful information to staff and visitors.

## Noise Control

Consideration should be given to the control of noise in the space for the automated function. Noise can be defined as any unwanted sound that interferes with one's concentration or serenity. Usually, noise is not a problem in libraries, due to the cultural feeling that the library is a place to be subdued and quiet. However, this is not always the case. Street noises, doors that close improperly, computer printers, idle chatter of people walking down trafficways, and other unintentional noise can be distracting and irritating to both staff and users alike. The trend to open office space also contributes to noise in the library workplace. Air flowing through the ducts of the air handling units of the building can mask some noise, but this sound should be kept at a low level so that it does not become a noise problem itself.

Much noise can be absorbed by fixed walls, if the walls are constructed to trap, rather than transmit, sound. Walls with air space between two partitions are best; walls also may be treated with a sound-absorbing covering. Walls built completely to the structural ceiling of the building will prevent sound from being transmitted to nearby areas or rooms.

Another technique of minimizing noise in the space for the automated function is through careful placement of its workstations. Space of more than three feet between them seems to be effective in controlling noise. Also, workstations should be placed to prevent lines of sight between them, if possible. That is, a person sitting at a workstation should not be able to see his or her neighbors at other workstations.

Still another technique of reducing noise in the space is to install an acoustical ceiling. Acoustic tiles, for example, can trap or scatter sound that otherwise would be reflected directly into workstations near the source of the noise. This type of treatment will be especially beneficial in reducing noise in an open plan arrangement.

Still another effective technique for controlling noise in open spaces is to use acoustical partitions or panels to separate workstations and other noise-producing elements of the automated system being implemented. Care should be taken to install panels constructed with a sound-absorbing inner structure, else little noise will be reduced. The panels should be of sufficient height and width to absorb the maximum amount of sound possible.

When noisy equipment, such as a computer printer, must be used at or near a workstation, a special acoustical hood or cover can be installed over the equipment to contain and reduce its noise. A pad can be placed under the printer to further reduce noise and vibration.

When possible, noisy equipment such as computer printers should be physically isolated from people. The equipment can be located as far away as possible from other workstations, either behind acoustical panels or in an enclosed room.

Floors of the workplace should be carpeted, particularly in the open plan concept. Carpeting absorbs impact noise such as footsteps and scraping chairs on the floor. A pad should be placed between the carpet and the floor, rather than gluing the carpet directly to the subfloor. Care should be taken that antistatic carpeting is chosen to eliminate or minimize damage to sensitive electronic equipment.

## IMPLEMENTATION SPECIFICATIONS

Specifications should be prepared for all construction and installation work and all items that must be purchased for the floorspace design implementation. These specifications will be used to prepare purchase orders, bid requisitions, or work requests when the plan is implemented.

The space planning and design team should gather or prepare specifications for construction and renovation, floor covering, partitions, and furniture.

### Construction and Renovation

Detailed specifications will be necessary if any construction or renovation of the space for the automated function is anticipated. The exact location of walls and doors should be shown on a scaled representation of the floorspace, preferably without workstations and other furniture and equipment shown. If a special construction method is necessary, such as plaster-on-lathe or sheetrock on 2″ by 4″ studs, this should be specified. The exact location of electrical outlets and the type of receptacle to be installed should be indicated. Paint chips for the colors of walls should be provided. If a new ceiling is to be installed, a tile sample should be made available. Specifications for the type of lighting fixtures and their locations should be detailed. If special window coverings are to be installed, specifications and colors should be provided. Other specifications, such as stripping existing carpeting from the subfloor or the application of graphics, should be described.

## Floor Covering

The type, quality, and color of floor covering for the space where the automated function will be housed must be specified. Tiles of various types, such as vinyl or rubber and carpeting, are common floor coverings used in libraries. Attention should be paid to durability, maintainability, and cost, as well as aesthetics and sound control. A constraint on the space planning and design team might be that the floor covering chosen must match that already used in adjacent areas of the building.

## Partitions

Specifications must be prepared for any movable partitions to be used in an open space planning concept for the automated function. The height, width, acoustic ability, type of covering, and color should be specified.

## Furniture

Detailed specifications will be necessary for all furniture such as desks, tables, chairs, filing cabinets, shelving, etc., for the design. The material to be used, size, construction methods, design, color, and quality must be specified.

## IMPLEMENTATION COSTS

The last step of space planning and design, before the team's report is written, should be the estimation of costs for implementing its recommendations. Many costs probably were determined as requirements of the automated function were studied and as specialists were consulted.

The team should gather estimated costs for:

- Construction and renovation of the quarters
- Purchase and installation of wiring and cabling
- Painting the workspace
- Upgrades for lighting
- Purchase and installation of carpeting
- Installation or relocation of telephones
- Purchase and installation of partitions
- Installation of computer terminals

- Purchase and installation of other equipment
- Purchase of furniture
- Moving expenses
- Miscellaneous expenses

## THE PLANNING AND DESIGN REPORT

A report of the space planning and design work should be prepared for submission to the manager of the automated function and others. The report will be used to assess the space planning and design team's work, decide whether or not to proceed with implementing the recommendations, and guide the implementation steps, once approved.

Information in the document should include, as a minimum, the planning and design goals and constraints, the requirements of the automated function for space, the workstation layouts, the workspace layout, specifications for furniture and equipment purchases, and the cost estimates for the design. Other background or explanatory information considered pertinent to improve the report can be included or appended.

The report should be neatly prepared and bound. A word processor is ideal for preparing the report, since this method will enable multiple drafts and corrections to be made easily and quickly. If the floorspace layouts are large, they may be separate from the rest of the report.

A draft of the report can be circulated to key staff before it is submitted for approval, to solicit suggestions and comments for improving the document and to gain their vital support for the design. Their suggestions should be evaluated carefully and, if possible, incorporated into the document before it is submitted formally for approval.

## ADDITIONAL READINGS

Anderson, John F., and others. *Library Space Planning.* New York: Library Journal, 1976.

Bennett, Corwin A. "Lighting." In *Handbook of Industrial Engineering,* edited by Gavriel Salvendy. New York: Wiley, 1982: 6.11.1-8.

———. *Spaces for People: Human Factors of Design.* Englewood Cliffs, NJ: Prentice-Hall, 1977.

Berkeley, Bernard. *Floors: Selection and Maintenance.* (Library Technology Publication 13). Chicago: American Library Association, 1969.

Birrin, Faber. *Color and Human Response.* New York: Van Nostrand Reinhold, 1978.

Brownrigg, Edwin B. "Library Automation: Building and Equipment Considerations in Implementing Computer Technology." In *Advances in Library Administration and Organization*, edited by Gerard B. McCabe, Bernard Kreissman, and W. Carl Jackson. Vol. 1. Greenwich, CT: JAI Press, 1982: 43-53.

Bush, Margaret A. "Space: Factors in Planning and Use." *Illinois Libraries* 60 (December 1978): 898-903.

Cerami and Associates, Inc. *Sound Control in the Open Office: A Guide to Speech Privacy*. Muskegon, MI: Shaw-Walker, 1979.

Channer, Stephen D. "The Case for Furniture Befitting the Human Condition." *Modern Office Procedure* (June 1983): 53-60.

Cochran, J. Wesley. "Integrating New Technology: Some Architectural Solutions." *Law Library Journal* 74 (Summer 1981): 643-53.

Cohen, Elaine, and Aaron Cohen. *Automation: Space Management, and Productivity: A Guide for Libraries*. New York: Bowker, 1981.

————. *Planning the Electronic Office*. New York: McGraw-Hill, 1983.

Corlett, E. Nigel. "Design of Handtools, Machines, and Workplaces." In *Handbook of Industrial Engineering*, edited by Gavriel Salvendy. New York: Wiley, 1982: 6.9.1-12.

Debear, R. "Planning the Electronic Library." *Managing the Electronic Library*. New York: Special Libraries Association, 1984: 26-32.

Drabenstott, Jon, ed. "Designing Library Facilities for a High-Tech Future." *Library Hi Tech* 5 (Winter 1987): 103-11.

Draper, James, and James Brooks. *Interior Design for Libraries*. Chicago: American Library Association, 1979.

Fraley, Ruth A., and Carol L. Anderson. *Library Space Planning: How to Assess, Allocate, and Reorganize Collections, Resources, and Physical Facilities*. New York: Neal-Schuman, 1985.

Hall, Richard B. "Library Space Utilization Methodology." *Library Journal* 103 (December 1, 1978): 2379-83.

Harris, David S., and others. *Planning and Designing the Office Environment*. New York: Van Nostrand Reinhold Company, 1981.

Herbert, R. Kring. "Noise Control in the Open Plan." *Administrative Management* (December 1980): 27-29.

Hildrich, Stephen R. "Problems of the Open Space Library." *Connecticut Libraries* 20 (Fall 1978): 42-44.

Hodge, M.P., and B. Lawrence. "Planning for the Electronic Library." In *Managing the Electronic Library*. New York: Special Libraries Association, 1984: 13-25.

*IES Lighting Handbook: 1984 Reference Volume*. New York: Illuminating Engineering Society of North America, 1984.

Isacco, Jeanne M. "Workspaces, Satisfaction, & Productivity in Libraries." *Library Journal* 110 (May 1, 1985): 27-30.

Lawrie, R.J. "Flexible Light and Power for Library Offices." *Electrical Construction and Maintenance* 76 (November 1977): 78-81.

Mariotti, John J. "Office Layout." In *Handbook of Industrial Engineering*, edited by Gavriel Salvendy. New York: Wiley, 1982: 10.6.1-20.

Metcalf, Keyes D. *Planning Academic and Research Library Buildings*, by Philip D. Leighton and David L. Weber. 2nd ed. Chicago: American Library Association, 1986.

Michaels, David Leroy. "Technology's Impact on Library Interior Planning." *Library Hi Tech* 5 (Winter 1987): 59-63.

Muther, Richard, and Lee Hales. "Six Steps To Making an Office Layout." *The Office* 85 (March 1977): 29-33.

Palmer, Alvin E., and M. Susan Lewis. *Planning the Office Landscape*. New York: McGraw-Hill, 1977.

Pennybaker, Ed. "Designing Facilities for a High-Tech Future: The OCLC Online Computer Center, Inc. Headquarters—A Case Study." *Library Hi Tech* 5 (Winter 1987): 41-48.

Pierce, William S. *Furnishing the Library Interior*. New York: Marcel Dekker, 1980.

Pulgram, William L., and Richard E. Stonis. *Designing the Automated Office: A Guide for Architects, Interior Designers, Space Planners, and Facility Managers*. New York: Whitney Library of Design, Watson-Guptill Publications, 1984.

Ridgeway, Patricia M. "Planning and Designing Library Floorplans." *Research Strategies* 3 (Summer 1985): 135-39.

Rosen, Harold J. *Construction Specifications Writing: Principles and Procedures*. New York: Wiley, 1974.

Schweigler, Peter. "Conventional Library Work in Administrative Libraries by Means of Modern Technology and Technical Equipment." *INSPEL* 18 (No.3, 1984): 162-93.

Selesner, Gary. "Furniture for the Electronic Office." *Office Product News* (April 1979): 7-10.

Steele, Fritz. *Making and Managing High-Quality Workplaces: An Organizational Ecology*. New York: Teachers College Press, 1986.

Tedesco, Eleanor Hollis, and Robert B. Mitchell. *Administrative Office Management: The Electronic Office*. New York: Wiley, 1984.

"Work Environment: Its Design and Implications." *Personnel Journal* 60 (January 1981): 27-31.

# Chapter 7
# Workstations

Much of the work in an automated library function will be performed at a workstation, located at the circulation desk, in a technical services area, or in a public area. This chapter discusses workstations for use in an automated library function. Specifically, its topics include:

- Workstation hardware
- Workstation desks
- Seating
- Lighting
- Workstation security
- Number of workstations required

## WORKSTATION HARDWARE

A *workstation* is a configuration of furniture and equipment organized and arranged for performance by an individual of one or more tasks in a function. The station may contain a device or series of devices from which a staff member or library user can send or receive information from the computer supporting an automated function for the purpose of performing a job. The devices in this workstation will provide the principal links between staff and the computer supporting the function, and, often, between the library user and services of the library. Other workstations will not contain computer terminal devices, but nonetheless should also be designed for effective use by staff or other users.

The hardware in a specific workstation will depend upon the needs of the automated function, the computer supporting the function, the specific application being implemented, the staffing patterns of the function, and the financial ability of the library to acquire the hardware. Hardware commonly found in workstations include CRT terminals, microcomputer terminals, printer terminals, output-only printers, optical scanners, communications devices, and other hardware.

## CRT Terminals

A common device found in a workstation is the Cathode Ray Tube or CRT Terminal. The CRT terminal, also called a Visual Display Unit (VDU) or Visual Display Terminal (VDT), is the most common type of computer terminal used today. It is an input-output device that enables an operator to enter commands, queries, and other information to be communicated from the workstation to the computer. Responses from the computer, such as the results of processing or a file search, are returned to the CRT terminal in the workstation. The operator and the computer can carry on an exchange of information or a dialogue in this manner, each interacting with the other as processing in the function progresses. The workstation and the computer may be hundreds of feet or hundreds of miles apart.

A CRT terminal consists of a cathode ray tube screen display or monitor and, usually, a keyboard which may or may not be detachable. The monitor comes in a variety of sizes, but 12-inch screens are most common. Usually, 25 lines of 80 characters each can be displayed. As a rule, applications with frequent screen proofreading or referencing dictates the use of a monochrome monitor. The keyboard is similar to that of a typewriter, but with some special function and control keys added. As it is keyed, information also is displayed on the terminal's monitor for visual verification and correction if necessary.

Some CRT terminals provided for use by the public have no keyboard for input of information. Rather, their screens contain sensitive touchpads that can be easily activated by touching the screen's surface. An operator merely touches a part of the screen containing information to send commands and queries to the computer for processing. Other CRT terminals have special keyboards designed for use by the public in searching an online catalog. For example, the Brodart Company provides a ten-key keypad for use with its Le Pac catalog. Still other terminals may have an extended keyboard providing the full ALA character set, diacritics, and special graphics features.

The operator will use a CRT terminal to enter commands, queries, and other information into the computer for processing or storage. The computer will use the terminal's monitor as a means to respond to commands and queries and return the results of processing and file searches and other information to the operator.

CRT terminals are classed as either "intelligent" or "dumb." Both types have their advantages and their limitations of use in automated library functions. An "intelligent" terminal has internal storage and the capability of performing limited computing, such as checking and editing information before it is transmitted to the computer for further processing. For example, the terminal may check a barcode for scanning errors, check a command for correctness, or delete punctuation and blanks in a search term before the information is sent to the computer. The intelligent terminal may also perform limited processing on information being returned by the computer before it is displayed on the CRT screen for the operator. For example, the terminal might add blanks to compacted information or might format information into a pleasing screen arrangement before it is displayed on the monitor. An advantage to using intelligent terminals in an automated library function is that they could relieve the computer system of some essential processing and, therefore, enable better response time to all terminals. A disadvantage is that intelligent terminals are more expensive than dumb ones—usually from two to three times more.

A "dumb" terminal, on the other hand, can itself process no information entered into it by an operator or returned to it by the computer system. It is designed only to transmit information to the computer for processing or storage and to display information received from the computer. An advantage to using dumb terminals in an automated library function is that these devices are inexpensive, thus enabling the library to afford more of them. A disadvantage is that, since the dumb terminal can perform no information processing, the computer itself must check, edit, convert, and organize all information transmitted to it or being returned to the terminal for display. This could reduce the response time to all terminals attached to the system.

## Microcomputer Terminals

Since the microcomputer is increasingly being used as either a stand-alone computer or as a terminal linked to one or more other microcomputers, minicomputers, or mainframe computers, a workstation might include a microcomputer terminal rather than a CRT terminal. The uses of the microcomputer terminal will be the same as for a CRT terminal.

Having a device that can serve both as a computer terminal when necessary and as a stand-alone microcomputer at other times can eliminate the need for separate devices for these differing functions. This can save both space and money for the library. A microcomputer used as a terminal in a workstation can provide access to several automated functions from the same location, which might enable an integration of information from several sources. For example, a workstation user may wish to download information or files from one automated function, manipulate the information, then merge the results with information from another function. This may not be possible using a standard computer terminal, but may be so using a microcomputer.

Using a microcomputer as a terminal in an automated library function requires that the machine have an adapter card in one of its expansion slots and terminal emulation software. When functioning as or emulating a computer terminal, the microcomputer may be either "intelligent" or "dumb," depending on the computer system and the application software to which it is to be connected. Different emulation methods require different microcomputer emulation hardware and software.

There can be some disadvantages or limitations to using a microcomputer as both a terminal to the computer supporting an automated function and as a stand-alone computer. Unless there truly is a need to access several computer systems at one location, using a microcomputer as a terminal may not be an acceptable alternative. Loading the terminal emulation software and connecting the microcomputer to the other computer supporting other automated functions may be a burden. There may be a tendency on the part of the staff to use the microcomputer exclusively as a terminal to one automated function, in which case the microcomputer's special capabilities may be wasted. If this is the case, a standard computer terminal may be a wiser and less expensive choice.

## Printer Terminals

Instead of either a CRT or a microcomputer terminal, a workstation might contain a printer terminal. The printer terminal once was the principal input-output device for online, interactive use of computers, but has been replaced almost entirely by the faster and more fashionable CRT or microcomputer terminal. Use of the printer terminal today in libraries is confined almost exclusively to online searching of remote databases. Even this use is declining in favor of the CRT terminal with an attached output or "slave" printer.

Most printer terminals are similar to an electric typewriter, but with a few additional keys and a pin-feed platen for use of continuous forms. The operator enters commands, queries, and other information through the keyboard. The information is printed on the paper in the device as information is keyed. The computer prints the results of its processing or responses to queries and commands on the same paper.

An advantage to using a printer terminal for accessing an automated library function is that a hardcopy record of all input and output is made automatically. A disadvantage is its slow speed.

## Output-Only Printers

A workstation might include a printer that is attached to or used with a computer terminal. The printer may be plugged into the printer or auxiliary port on the back of a CRT or microcomputer terminal. In some cases, it may be completely independent of a terminal, being connected to the computer in a manner similar to other terminals.

A printer as part of a computer workstation could have several uses. One use might be to generate, upon demand, purchase orders, overdue notices, date-due slips, receipts, statistical reports, and other documents as an automated function is operated. In this manner, the staff need not wait for an overnight batch job to provide documents and reports. There is no need to walk to a distant computer room to get output documents and reports, because they are prepared at the workstation, when and where they are needed.

Another use for an output-only printer in a workstation might be to print the same information that is being displayed on the screen of a CRT or microcomputer terminal. This is useful when a hardcopy of information being displayed is needed to document something or to continue a process away from the workstation. For example, staff may want a hardcopy of a record being displayed to take to the shelflist or to a bibliographic source to verify and correct its information. Still another use might be to print receipts during charging and discharging in an automated circulation function or during the receipt of materials in an automated acquisitions function.

Any one of several types of printers could be used in a workstation. Fully-formed character printers are best when letter-quality output is required. Fully-formed characters resemble those in a typewriter. Dot-matrix printers, which form characters by printing a number of small dots to form a character image, are satisfactory for most other printing. An impact type printer must be used when multi-part forms are to be produced in order that the characters can be transferred to the different copies of the form. When both high quality and quietness are desired, a non-impact ink jet or laser printer can be used.

## Optical Scanners

A workstation might include an optical scanner attached to the CRT or microcomputer terminal. The scanner will be used to enter information stored in the form of barcodes or Optical Character Recognition (OCR) characters into the computer for processing. The scanned information is displayed on the monitor of the computer terminal for visual verification. Optical scanning, which is rapid and avoids manual keyboarding, is commonly used in an automated circulation function to enter borrower and material identification numbers into the system and in acquisitions and cataloging functions to enter material identification numbers as search terms during file searching.

There are several types of optical scanners for use in a workstation. One type is the wand or pencil scanner, and another is the gun scanner. Both are handheld and work in a similar manner, using infrared light. A more sophisticated and expensive laser scanner, which sits stationary near a workstation, is available. The scanners usually are plugged into an interface port on the back of the CRT or microcomputer terminal.

## Communications Devices

A workstation might include one or more communications devices, such as a modem and/or a telephone, for its proper use and operation. A modem is a device that accepts digital information from a CRT, microcomputer, or printer terminal and transforms the signal into a form suitable for transmission over a communications facility such as a telephone line. This device will be necessary when a computer terminal in the workstation is located at a distance from the computer supporting an automated function. The modem probably will be positioned where it will be out of the way of the workstation user. For example, the device may be placed on a shelf underneath the station. A telephone may be necessary in a workstation, either for voice communications or for data transmission, or for both uses.

## Other Hardware

Some operations may not require staff to have access to the computer supporting an automated library function, and therefore will not require computer-related hardware in the workstation. In some cases, no equipment at all will be necessary, while some workstations will require a typewriter, a calculator, or other electronic or mechanical equipment. This type of workstation nonetheless should be carefully designed for optimum efficiency of staff or other users.

## WORKSTATION DESKS

A workstation for an automated library function will require a table or desk to house the computer hardware and other essential devices and equipment and to provide workspace for using the equipment and performing other tasks. The operator may sit, stand, or alternately sit and stand while using the workstation.

## Styles and Types of Desks

Several styles and types of desks are available for use in a workstation. The type of desk chosen will depend upon the functions to be performed in the workstation, the equipment to be used, and the space layout chosen for the automated system as discussed in Chapter 6.

The desk can be single pedestal containing storage drawers on one side only, double pedestal containing storage drawers on both sides, or with no drawers. Returns or side workspaces may be used with the single-pedestal or no-pedestal desk.

## Work Surface Heights

The workstation table or desk should reflect the needs of the person or persons using it, allowing him or her to work comfortably with minimum fatigue. For tasks to be performed while seated, the work surface height should be from 27 to 28 inches from the floor. Adjustable work surface heights from 23 to 30 inches should be provided if possible. Some tables designed for CRT use allow the part holding the device's keyboard to be adjusted separately from the remainder of the surface. In this way, the workstation can be used comfortably by a number of operators through adjustment of the seating, the keyboard height, and the angle of the CRT screen.

For those working in a standing position, such as at a circulation desk or an online public access catalog terminal, the work surface should be from 36 to 41 or 42 inches from the floor for males and from 33 to 38 inches for females. Since these stations will be used by both males and females and the heights of most standing stations are not adjustable, an average work surface from 36 to 38 inches from the floor may be satisfactory.

Space for work forms and other documents and supplies should be provided at each side of a CRT terminal, thereby supporting the needs of both right- and left-handed operators. Most operators prefer to have work copy directly in front of them, positioned below the screen and above the keyboard of the device. This configuration allows easy eye movement from the copy to the screen without the strain of turning the head to the right or left to view documents.

## SEATING

Proper seating is probably one of the most important components of the workstation. The chair must adjust not only to the height of a computer keyboard and screen and documents and other items on the work surface, but also to the weight distribution and posture requirements of the operator.

## Seat Height

The height of the seat should be adjustable so that the thighs of a person remain at a 90-degree angle to the floor with the feet flat on the floor to avoid excessive pressure on the thighs. Heights adjustable from 15 to 19 inches should be sufficient. Fixed-seat height should be approximately 17 inches from the floor.

## Seat Depth, Width, and Angle

The depth of the seat should not exceed 17 inches, and the width not less than 16 inches. A forward-sloping seat pan, with the back edge of the seat approximately three degrees higher than the front edge, will improve curvature of the spine. This is important when a person must lean forward while performing assigned tasks.

## Backrest

In order to provide firm support for the lower back, the seat back should be adjustable up and down and should tilt back and forth.

## Angles for CRT Use

The CRT screen should be positioned so that the operator's head can remain level and the display can be viewed at approximately 15 degrees below eye level. The operator should be able to adjust the screen up and down and to the left and right to suit personal preference angles and to eliminate glare from light sources. The keyboard should be at a height that enables the operator's elbows to remain at a 90 degree angle and the wrists straight rather than angled downward or upward. For the average operator, this will mean a keyboard height from the floor of approximately 26 inches.

## LIGHTING

Lighting level and glare are two important aspects of illumination for a workstation. The proper level of illumination for work at CRT terminals is controversial, with various experts recommending differing values. However, it is agreed that a "reasonable" level of general illumination is necessary for the work area. The *IES Lighting Handbook* should be consulted for specific standards of lighting.

Glare from windows and ceiling lights on the terminal screen and work documents should be minimized as much as possible. The workstation should be located away from windows, or if this is not possible or desirable, the windows should be shaded. The display screen can be tilted to reduce glare from overhead lighting. Shields and mesh covering the screen can reduce glare further.

## WORKSTATION SECURITY

The two concerns regarding workstation security are unauthorized access to activities and files and the physical safety of equipment.

### Unauthorized Access to Activities and Files

A common problem in an automated library function is how to restrict unauthorized access to activities and files from workstations containing a computer terminal. There are three common means of achieving this. The method used will depend upon the design of the automated function and the software supporting the application.

One method is to allow only designated functions and files to be accessed from specific terminals in workstations. For example, public workstations with computer terminals may be restricted to accessing only an online catalog, or workstations in the circulation department may be allowed access only to the automated circulation function. In some systems, activities or features will not appear in a menu displayed at a workstation if access to them is not allowed. In other systems, a function might not appear in the menu selection list display at a workstation terminal, but might be accessible by authorized staff using hidden commands that must be entered through the keyboard.

Another common means of controlling access in an automated function is to assign passwords to staff authorized to use specific activities and files. In order to gain access to an activity or a file, a person would enter a password. The computer would check its files to determine that the password is valid and which activities and files the person is authorized to use. The computer would permit the person access only to those authorized in its password file. The ability to perform specific functions also can be controlled by the computer. For example, a person may be authorized to view a file, but not update it. Or a person may be allowed to add information to a file, but not change or delete records. In this manner, access to and control of the automated function can be determined by each individual's need to use activities and files. The passwords can be purged or changed periodically, to minimize security problems.

A third method of restricting access to activities and files is to place a cover over the keyboard of a workstation. The cover hooks over the keyboard and can be locked. This can be an inexpensive solution to a security problem, but will be useful only in limited circumstances.

## The Physical Safety of Equipment

It is unfortunate that some libraries must protect their computer equipment from vandalism and theft. However, in many situations, this is necessary. Several security techniques are available.

One of the best deterrents to loss and vandalism of staff equipment is to restrict unauthorized people from the areas where workstations are located. Locking doors to restricted areas is the best method. If this is impossible at all times, locking staff areas where and when workstations are left unattended is an alternative method.

Another method of maximizing the physical safety of the equipment is to place public terminals near service points where staff can observe their use. Even if the workstations cannot and will not be watched constantly, the proximity of staff can be a deterrent to vandalism and theft. When workstations cannot be placed within sight of a service point, they should be placed in areas where there is as much user traffic as possible.

Still another means of ensuring the physical safety of equipment is to bolt or chain devices to tables or desks. Alarms can be installed that will sound if anyone tampers with the security devices. If the library has a security system, targets can be placed in or on the pieces of equipment so that alarms will sound if someone attempts to take them through the security gate.

## THE NUMBER OF WORKSTATIONS REQUIRED

The number of workstations needed in an automated library function will depend upon such factors as the need of staff to access the computer system, the frequency of access, and the volume of work requiring access. Those activities with the highest need for access to the computer and the largest workload should be allocated one or more terminals. For example, those staff in an automated circulation function who are responsible for checking out materials need continual access to a terminal during the hours the library is open. If the circulation level is high, more than one terminal may be necessary to minimize the waiting time of borrowers to check out materials.

While each staff member ideally could have a computer terminal at his or her assigned workspace, space and financial limitations will usually make this impossible. Therefore, several staff usually must share the same terminal, either on a first-come or a scheduled basis. In many cases, different operations can be performed at the same computer terminal. For example, charging materials and borrower registration may be performed at the same station. If only a few terminals are available to an automated function, several activities may have to share the same station. For example, the reserves, holds and recalls, and fines activities may all use the same computer terminal. In the very small library, all computer tasks may be performed at the same terminal.

A technique of determining an adequate number of computer terminal workstations for the staff is to initially provide a reasonable number, then carefully schedule their use by staff so that the equipment is in use throughout each work day. If staff cannot complete their required work in the time allowed, more workstations are added. One station should be added at a time until all staff required to use the automated system have sufficient time each day to complete their work.

Various formulas and rules of thumb have been suggested for determining the number of public use workstations such as those for searching a library's online catalog. One technique is to use queuing models to determine the number needed. The models require that data, such as the number of persons entering the library, the number of terminals in use at different times of the day, and the length of time users spend at terminals, be collected and applied against a mathematical queuing model. The result will be the number of terminals that should serve peak-time usage with minimum waiting time to use a station. A less-demanding, and perhaps as accurate, method is to provide a reasonable number of public terminals initially, watch for congestion during the peak library usage hours, and increase the number of stations until the peak-time demand is met. A balance between too few and too many workstations can be determined by observing their use at a variety of times each day over a period of time such as several months.

The number of computer terminal workstations considered necessary to support an automated function may not be the number allotted to it. The allotment will depend upon the number of terminals the computer supporting the function can accommodate, the number of other automated functions sharing the same computer and their need for terminals, and the ability of the library to purchase terminals. But space planning and design should be conducted on the basis of the number of computer terminal workstations *needed* by the automated system, not the number allotted to it. If more terminals are required than are available initially, space should be planned for the larger number, on the assumption that additional devices will be added at a later time.

Some workstations without computer terminals may be required in an automated function. For example, for processing overdue notices in an automated circulation function, only a table or desk might be required, since the remaining steps to be completed after the computer produces the notices are to check, separate, and place the forms in mailing envelopes. Management staff, secretaries, and other support staff who do not require access to the computer in their assigned work will require workstations without computer terminals. Also, staff who do need computer access will need to retreat from working at computer terminals for a part of each workday. Staff cannot work at a terminal more than two or three consecutive hours at a time without serious eyestrain and fatigue. Workstations, which might be standard desks without computer terminals, provide a place for staff to perform other assigned duties away from the computer.

## ADDITIONAL READINGS

Borgman, Christine, and Neal K. Kaske. "Determining the Number of Terminals Required for an On-Line Catalog Through Queueing Analysis of Catalog Traffic Data." In *Clinic on Library Applications of Data Processing, 17th: 1980.* Champaign, IL: University of Illinois at Urbana-Champaign, 1981: 20-36.

Brooks, Tom, ed. *The Local Area Network Reference Guide.* Englewood Cliffs, NJ: Prentice-Hall, 1985.

Bube, Judith L. "The Application of Ergonomic Principles to VDT Workstations." *Technicalities* 6 (November 1986): 9-12.

Cakir, A., D.J. Hart, and T.F.M. Steward. *Visual Display Terminals: A Manual Covering Ergonomics, Workplace Design, Health and Safety, Task Organization.* New York: Wiley, 1980.

Christie, Linda Gail. *The Simon and Schuster Guide to Computer Peripherals.* New York: Simon and Schuster, 1985.

Corbin, John. "Terminal Work Stations." In *Managing the Library Automation Project.* Phoenix: Oryx Press, 1985: 141-43.

Dainoff, M.J. "Learning From Office Automation: Ergonomics and Human Impact." In *Clinic on Library Applications of Data Processing, 22nd: 1985.* Champaign, IL: University of Illinois at Urbana-Champaign, 1986: 16-29.

Eastman Kodak Company. The Human Factors Section. Health, Safety and Human Factors Laboratory. *Ergonomic Design for People at Work.* (Vol.1: Workplace, Equipment, and Environmental Design and Information Transfer). Belmont, CA: Lifetime Learning Publications, 1983.

Edmunds, Robert A. *The Prentice-Hall Encyclopedia of Information Technology.* Englewood Cliffs, NJ: Prentice-Hall, 1987.

Human Factors Society. *American National Standard for Human Factors Engineering of Visual Display Terminal Workstations.* Santa Monica, CA: Human Factors Society, 1985.

Johnson, James K. "Touching Data." *Datamation* 23 (January 1977): 70-72.

Mason, Robert M. "Ergonomics: The Human and the Machine." *Library Journal* 109 (February 15, 1984): 331-32.

Michaels, Andrea. "Design Today." *Wilson Library Bulletin* 62 (September 1987): 56-59.

Pheasant, Stephen. *Bodyspace: Anthropometry, Ergonomics, and Design.* Philadelphia: Taylor & Francis, 1986.

Roose, T. "Ergonomics in the Library." *Library Journal* 111 (October 15, 1986): 54-55.

Sage, Charles, and others. "A Queuing Study of Public Catalog Use." *College & Research Libraries* 42 (July 1981): 317-25.

Tijerina, L. *Video Display Terminal Workstation Ergonomics.* Dublin, OH: OCLC, 1984.

Tolle, John E., Nancy P. Sanders, and Neal K. Kaske. "Determining the Required Number of Online Catalog Terminals: A Research Study." *Information Technology and Libraries* 2 (September 1983): 261-65.

# Chapter 8
# Documentation for the
# Automated Function

A set of documentation must be developed and made available to the staff of the automated library function. This material will be in the form of narrative and pictorial descriptions of various aspects of the automated function, manuals, and other documents. The information will be used by library staff and others during their education and training, for reference purposes after the education and training, for quality control purposes, and for other uses as the function is operated and managed. Documentation for the automated function should be revised as often as is necessary to keep the information current and relevant.

In this chapter, the minimum documentation needed to support the automated function is discussed. Specifically, the chapter includes discussions of:

- General descriptive information
- Organizational charts
- Job descriptions
- Equipment descriptions
- Procedure manuals
- Policy manuals
- Computer operations documentation

## GENERAL DESCRIPTIVE INFORMATION

One type of documentation that should be developed and made available is general descriptive information about the automated library function. This information will provide background and an overview of the function and its various aspects; it will be used by the staff as a part of their orientation to the system and to their new duties and responsibilities. General descriptive information also can be used for reference purposes at any future time.

## Content

General descriptive information for an automated function can consist of several parts, including:

1. A summary or overview of the overall design of the automated function, including its general capabilities and limitations.
2. A summary or overview description of each component activity and each specific feature of the automated function, including their general capabilities and limitations.
3. A summary or overview of the computer system supporting the automated function.
4. A profile of the company or vendor supplying the software supporting the automated function.

## Preparation

In order to prepare general descriptive information, the librarian will have to collect documents, reports, and pieces of information from various sources, then synthesize, summarize, and edit the information into a form that will be useful to the staff of the automated function. Some information can be found in brochures and other literature published by the company or firm vending the software and hardware, while other information must be created from scratch or from various other miscellaneous sources.

## Format and Availability

Since general descriptive information for the automated function should be short and not subject to drastic change over time, it can be typed and stapled together or placed in binders. A title page and table of contents can be supplied. Several options are available for making general descriptive information available to the staff of the automated function. If the documentation is small and easily duplicated, a copy should be given each staff member. If the staff is large and the documentation cannot be duplicated easily, then at least one copy can be deposited in each organizational unit of the function. If possible, a copy should be placed at each workstation in the function. It might be possible to place one or more copies in a clearly-marked and easily-accessible location available to all staff. For the small staff, one copy of the information might suffice.

## ORGANIZATIONAL CHARTS

Another document that should be made available to all staff is an organizational chart for the automated library function. This chart will be a useful aid for visualizing the organizational structure of the function and its activities, management structure, and lines of authority, to enable the staff to understand relationships within the function. This will be particularly important when existing staff are learning their new roles and responsibilities in the automated function. To the new staff member, the chart can provide an easy and rapid means of obtaining an overview of the component parts of the function and how they interrelate with each other. A copy of the organizational chart should be given to each staff member of the automated function. The chart should be revised and re-issued from time to time as changes in the organization are made.

## JOB DESCRIPTIONS

Another type of documentation that should be made available to the staff who will be working in the automated library function is the job description. Individual staff members will use the job descriptions as a guide and reference to their new duties and responsibilities, and they also will be used by managers within the function in the recruitment, training, and evaluation of staff.

Each staff member should have a copy of his or her own job description, and each manager or supervisor should have a copy of the job description for each employee he or she supervises. If possible, online copies of all job descriptions should be made available to facilitate the updating of the descriptions. Printouts of the descriptions should be available upon demand. The content and format of job descriptions were discussed in Chapter 5.

## EQUIPMENT DESCRIPTIONS

Descriptions of the equipment the staff will be using as they work in the automated library function should be provided. This documentation will be used during the initial orientation of the staff, during their individual training, and later as a reference guide when refresher information is needed.

### Content

Equipment descriptions can consist of several parts, including:

1. A general statement of the purpose of each piece of equipment and how it will be used in the automated function.

2. A description of the parts of the equipment and the purpose of each part.
3. A step-by-step procedure for turning on, operating, and turning off the equipment.
4. Procedures for troubleshooting problems with the equipment.
5. Procedures for cleaning the equipment.

A liberal use of photographs, line drawings, or other pictorial representations accompanying the documentation will be helpful to staff in visualizing the narrative descriptions.

## Preparation

Manuals, brochures, and other literature supplied by the manufacturers or vendors of equipment can be collected and used in preparing equipment descriptions for staff. In some cases, the staff can use the information provided by manufacturers and vendors without change. In other cases, the information provided is so technical or poorly organized and written that rewriting is necessary before it is given to the staff for their use.

## Format and Availability

Descriptions of equipment can be placed in a ring binder or other type of binder that will maintain the material together without loss and that can be updated easily by removing or inserting new documents or pages as the need arises. A title page and table of contents can be supplied, with tab dividers inserted between the sections or documents.

Copies of equipment descriptions can be placed at each workstation in the automated function. If the staff is small and workstations are located together physically, then one copy may suffice. If possible, the information can be placed online, as part of the Help Information System provided to equipment operators.

## PROCEDURE MANUALS

A manual of procedures to be followed when using the automated library function is essential. The manual will be used during orientation and training of staff for their new duties and responsibilities and for reference purposes during operation of the function, when staff forget a procedure and need refresher instructions. This documentation also enables a consistency in the training of staff and in the preferred method of performing operations.

## Content

The manual should include the step-by-step procedures for each activity of the automated function. Flow charts accompanying the procedures can be helpful to the staff in their visualization. Procedures to follow when problems arise with the hardware or software should also be included. For example, procedures to follow when cables become disconnected, a fuse blows, the software suddenly stops in the middle of a transaction, the power fails, etc., can be described.

## Preparation

Typically, procedures are written by the developer of the software supporting the automated function and provided to the library upon installation of the system. However, these manuals often pertain only to those aspects of the function supported by the computer. Many other procedures must be followed when performing other functions. Therefore, most procedure manuals supplied by software developers must be enhanced or supplemented to include those procedures not included and must be further customized for local conditions. Staff should have to refer to only one procedures manual for information about the operation of all activities of the automated function, whether or not functions are directly supported by the computer.

## Format and Availability

The procedure manual should also be housed in a ring binder so that the material can be retained together easily without loss and so that pages can be updated easily by removing or inserting new pages as the need arises. A title page and table of contents can be supplied, with tab dividers inserted between procedures for different activities or tasks within activities. Since procedure manuals usually are bulky, costly, and difficult to update, few copies can be prepared and maintained. At least one copy should be maintained in each organizational unit of the automated function.

If desired, separate procedure manuals can be provided for each activity of the automated function. For example, procedures for charging and renewing materials in an automated circulation function may be issued separately from procedures for handling overdues. Thus, those staff not involved with procedures in other organizational units of the automated function will not have copies of procedures for other units. In this case, a copy of all procedures should be retained in one manual, for those who do wish to refer to other procedures. The function's manager may wish to have a copy of all procedures in one manual. If possible, some or all of the procedures might be placed online, to be accessed through the Help Information System of the software supporting the automated function.

## POLICY MANUAL

A policy manual for the automated library function should be prepared. This important documentation will be referred to by managers within the function and other staff as the function is operated.

### Preparation

Policies for this manual can be drafted, discussed, re-written as necessary, and approved at any time during implementation of the automated function, or afterwards.

### Format and Availability

The policies pertaining to the automated function should be placed in a ring binder or other type of binder that will maintain the material together without loss and that can be updated easily by removing or inserting new policies. A title page and table of contents can be supplied, with tab dividers inserted between the policies.

## COMPUTER OPERATIONS DOCUMENTATION

Documentation for those who will operate and manage the computer system supporting the automated library function is vital. This material includes training, procedure, and policy manuals similar to those described above. Computer operations are discussed in Chapter 10.

## ADDITIONAL READINGS

Clayton, Marlene. "Documentation." In *Managing Library Automation*. London: Gower, 1987: 177-82.

Corbin, John. "Documentation Requirements." In *Managing the Library Automation Project*. Phoenix: Oryx Press, 1985: 91-92.

Long, L.F. *Data Processing Documentation and Procedures Manual*. Reston, VA: Reston Publishing Co., 1979.

Saffady, William. "Maintenance and Documentation." *Introduction to Automation for Librarians*. Chicago: American Library Association, 1983: 58-62.

# Chapter 9
# Database Conversion

Machine-readable information is an indispensable element of any auto-mated library function. Some information, such as that found in cir-culation and acquisitions transactions, can be automatically generated in machine-readable form as automated functions are operated on a day-to-day basis. But other information, in bibliographic and copy records, for example, must be converted to a machine-readable format before an automated function can be activated.

This chapter discusses the five typical files that must be converted to a machine-readable form before automated library functions can operate properly. These are:

- Bibliographic files
- Copy files
- Borrower files
- Vendor files
- Fund accounting files

## BIBLIOGRAPHIC FILES

A bibliographic file contains records describing materials in a library's collections, for cataloging, indexing, and accountability pur-poses. A record is required for each bibliographic title in the library's collection. The bibliographic file is created and maintained by the acquisitions and cataloging functions and utilized by the circulation function, an online public access catalog, and other activities. The same bibliographic file can be shared by all these functions.

The bibliographic records should be in the MARC format, to facilitate their compatibility with other libraries. Using this standard format is particularly important when the library is building its bib-liographic file and must rely on others as a source of machine-readable records. This compatibility will also be important should the library wish to join in cooperative programs with other libraries involving the exchange of bibliographic information.

In converting a bibliographic file to a machine-readable form, several steps are necessary.

## Identifying Options for Record Conversion

One of the first steps for converting bibliographic records to a machine-readable form is to identify the options open to the library. Several options for record conversion are available. Variations on each method might be possible.

*Option 1.* One option for converting the library's bibliographic records to a machine-readable form is to use a bibliographic utility such as OCLC. The following steps describe this option.

1. The library staff takes its shelf list trays to a terminal that can access the bibliographic utility's database.
2. The staff searches the database for matches to the shelflist records.
3. When potential matches are located, information in the database records is verified against that in the shelflist records. The staff edits located records to match the shelf list records.
4. The staff informs the utility's computer that edited records are acceptable, which triggers the addition of the library's holding symbol to the records in the bibliographic utility's database and the addition of copies of the edited records to a file that later will be transferred to magnetic tape, then sent to the library.
5. The staff marks the shelflist cards with a symbol indicating that conversion has been completed. Records not located in the bibliographic utility's database can be reviewed, tagged for input, and entered into the database as original cataloging. Copies of the machine-readable records also will be included on the magnetic tape sent later to the library.
6. Periodically, the bibliographic utility sends a magnetic tape of all records processed by the library during a period of time such as a month or a quarter.

The library usually pays a charge to the bibliographic utility for each record produced. The utility may have a special rate for bibliographic record conversion projects. Additional fees may be charged by the utility for each copy of a record sent to the library on magnetic tape, for the tape itself, and for shipping and handling.

A variation on this option is to electronically transfer copies of edited records directly into a local bibliographic file mounted on a computer system. This variation will ensure that records are immediately available locally and will eliminate the cost of the magnetic tape records. However, the library must have the appropriate cabling between the bibliographic utility terminal and the local computer system and software running on its computer to accommodate the process.

The advantages of this option are that a large percentage of the library's records can be located in the utility's database and accepted with little or no editing; the machine-readable records will be relatively error free when received on magnetic tape, because the library's staff will have edited and performed quality checks on each record as it was processed; and the library's holdings will be reflected in the utility's database for interlibrary loan and other cooperative ventures.

The disadvantages of this are that the library must supply the staff to process the shelflist cards against the utility's database, and those records not located in the utility's database must be specially processed and input manually.

*Option 2.* A second option for converting bibliographic records to a machine-readable form is to use a general database of bibliographic records stored on a medium such as CD-ROM. The following steps describe this option.

1. The library acquires the general bibliographic database on CD-ROM, a CD-ROM player, and a microcomputer.
2. The library staff takes its shelflist trays to the workstation and searches the database on CD-ROM for matches to the shelf list records.
3. When potential matches are located, a copy of the record is loaded into a local file and information in the database records is verified against that in the shelflist records. The staff edits located records to match the shelflist records.
4. In some CD-ROM systems, the library must order copies of located records from the vendor supplying the CD-ROM database. When a potential match to a shelflist record is located, the staff indicates that it wishes to purchase a copy of the machine-readable record. This request is stored on a diskette which is sent to the vendor when it is full of requests. The vendor then sends to the library a magnetic tape containing the machine-readable records.
5. The staff marks the shelflist cards with a symbol indicating that conversion has been completed. Records not located in the CD-ROM database must be converted using another method. In some systems, the software supplied with the CD-ROM database will allow the keying of full records from scratch.

The library must purchase or lease the bibliographic database on CD-ROM and the CD-ROM player and the microcomputer system. An additional cost per record extracted from the database for use in the local bibliographic file may be charged. No other fees usually are incurred.

The advantages of this option are that a large percentage of the library's records can be located in the CD-ROM database and accepted with little or no editing, and the machine-readable records will be relatively error free because the library's staff will have edited and performed quality checks on each record as it was processed.

The disadvantages of this option are that the library must supply the staff to process the shelflist cards against the CD-ROM database, additional equipment must be purchased by the library, those records not located in the database must be specially processed and input manually, and the records for those titles converted via this option will not automatically be reflected as being owned by the library in the database of a bibliographic utility, such as OCLC, for interlibrary loan and other cooperative ventures.

*Option 3.* A third option for bibliographic conversion is to request and purchase copies of the machine-readable records from a vendor. The following steps describe this option.

1. The library negotiates a contract with a vendor for the purchase of machine-readable bibliographic records.
2. The library acquires a microcomputer and special software for requesting records. The vendor might supply the software and perhaps loan one or more microcomputers to the library for the duration of the project.
3. The library staff takes its shelflist trays to the microcomputer and keys onto diskettes the LC Card Numbers, ISBN/ISSNs, or other identifying information for the records they wish to acquire.
4. When the library has filled several diskettes with requests for records, it sends the diskettes to the vendor.
5. The vendor compares the library's requests against its bibliographic database. Copies of bibliographic records that match the library's requests are placed on magnetic tape and returned to the library.

The library usually pays only a charge to the vendor for each record located and sent on magnetic tape. Sometimes, a processing fee and the cost of the the magnetic tape and its shipping and handling are charged.

The advantages of this option are that a large percentage of the library's records can be converted in a short period of time, and the library need devote only a small number of staff to prepare the requests for records.

The disadvantages of this option are that the records purchased from the vendor may require additional editing after they are received by the library, a percentage of records will be unavailable through the vendor and must be converted manually for an additional fee by the vendor or locally by the library's own staff, and the records for those titles converted via this option will not automatically be reflected as being owned by the library in the database of a bibliographic utility, such as OCLC, for interlibrary loan and other cooperative ventures.

*Option 4.* A fourth and last option for converting bibliographic records to a machine-readable form is to contract with a vendor to complete the entire conversion process. The following steps describe this option.

1. The library negotiates a contract with a vendor for the conversion process.
2. The library sends its shelflist, either all at once or several trays at a time, to the vendor.
3. The vendor's staff converts the records, either using its own in-house bibliographic database or that of a bibliographic utility. If machine-readable records are not located, the vendor's staff converts them manually.
4. The vendor returns the shelflist trays and the machine-readable records on magnetic tape to the library.

The library pays a per-record fee for the conversion. Higher costs must be expected when records must be converted manually.

The advantages of this option are that the library need not hire, train, and supervise additional staff or train and supervise existing staff for the conversion, the library need not purchase special equipment of any kind for its conversion project, and the vendor can complete the project much faster than could the library using other methods.

The disadvantages of this option are that the library would have to operate without its shelflist for the duration of the conversion, and the holdings converted under this option would not automatically be reflected as being owned by the library in the database of the bibliographic utility, such as OCLC, for interlibrary loan and other cooperative ventures.

## Selecting an Option for Conversion

Once the viable options for conversion have been identified, one method must be chosen. The option chosen will depend upon the staff available to the library for a conversion project, the time frame for conversion deemed necessary by the library, and the costs of the options.

A cost study of each option should be prepared. Consideration should be given by the library to the following cost elements:

1. Library staff costs of searching and editing records found in a bibliographic database, or of preparing requests for records to submit to a vendor.

2. The direct cost of each machine-readable record.
3. The cost of each machine-readable record received on magnetic tape, if not included in #2 above. The cost of the magnetic tape, shipping, and handling should be included.
4. Library staff costs, if any, of cleaning up records once they have been loaded into the local bibliographic file.

## Converting the Bibliographic Records

The next step is the actual conversion of bibliographic records to a machine-readable form, following the option selected by the library. The conversion project might take several months or several years, depending upon the number of records to be converted, the method chosen for conversion, and the need of the library for speed in converting its records.

## Pre-Processing the Records before Loading

Additional computer processing might be necessary before bibliographic records can be loaded into local computer storage for use by an automated library function such as circulation or an online public access catalog. Usually, the library will wait until most or all of its bibliographic records have been converted to a machine-readable form before this additional processing is done, as a last step before records are loaded into the local bibliographic file.

Possible additional record processing needed by the library includes the following:

1. Merging of records from various magnetic tape files into one file and eliminating duplicate records.
2. Automatically creating copy records. If additional information is made available, the computer can create a record for each copy of a library's holdings and append the copy record to, or incorporate it within, the machine-readable bibliographic record. This process is described further later in this chapter.
3. Checking and correcting filing indicators. The computer can check that filing indicators in the MARC record are set correctly and, if not, correct them.
4. Checking and correcting other specific information. The computer can check that specific tags are present and correct, change incorrect tags to correct ones, check that fixed fields are present and set in specific ways, perform the AACR-2 flip, and so on.

5. Matching specific headings against an authority file and correcting or supplying verified headings and cross-references.
6. Formatting or reformatting the bibliographic records according to the library's specifications prior to their loading into local computer storage.

## Loading the Records

The next step is for the library to load the processed, machine-readable bibliographic records into local computer storage, using the software written by or for the library or supplied by the vendor of the automated system. These records will comprise the library's base or initial load, which will be supplemented later as new machine-readable bibliographic records for newly acquired and cataloged materials, or as records not in machine-readable form, are converted and added.

As records are loaded into the local bibliographic file, either in batches or individually from an online interface with a bibliographic utility, some computer checking must take place. To accommodate the checking, the library must establish a profile of what it considers to be a good bibliographic record. This profile will contain a list of all tags, subfield codes, and other field codes and symbols that constitute a record in the library's internal format. If specific tags or data must be present for a record to be accepted, this must be stipulated. In many cases, the library must specify what constitutes valid data in some specific fields of a record.

Each bibliographic record loaded into the local computer system will be matched by the computer against the profile to determine that all required tags, codes, and other data are present and correct. Records with all required elements and correct data can be loaded into the bibliographic file, but those with requisite parts missing or containing tags or codes not specified in the profile may be held in a work file or tagged until corrections can be made by the library staff.

The computer should report problems encountered during loading the records into the bibliographic file to the staff for review and correction. Problems can be reported through a printout or an online display or a combination of both printed and online reports. The operator then adds missing data, tags, or codes, corrects errors as appropriate, or approves data that the software thought questionable. The corrected records may be matched once again against the library's bibliographic record profile to detect further anomalies. If additional errors are detected, the records appear on another problem report, but if no errors are detected, the records may be loaded into the bibliographic file.

The computer can detect errors in tags and codes and in fixed fields, but it cannot detect errors in the bibliographic information itself.

If errors are later detected after records have been loaded into the bibliographic file, the record can be displayed on a CRT screen for updating by the staff. The correct information then replaces the incorrect information.

## Indexing the Records

The last step might be to index the records in the local bibliographic file, using software written by or for the library or supplied by the vendor of the automated system. Common indexes for a bibliographic file, to support an online public access catalog or automated acquisitions and circulation function, include author; title; subject; author-title combination; keywords in authors, titles, and subjects; call number; LC Card Number; and ISBN/ISSN.

The library must define which data fields and subfields of the bibliographic records are to be included in each index.

> *Example*: MARC tags 100, 110, and 111 should be included in the author index. MARC tags 240 and 245 should be in the title index. MARC tags 600, 610, 611, 630, 650, 690, 691, 692, 693, 694, and 695 should be included in the subject index.

## COPY FILES

An item or copy file, which contains a record of each copy of a bibliographic title owned by the library, will be required by an automated circulation function and an online public access catalog. Copy records can be incorporated within their corresponding bibliographic records or can be in a separate file, with electronic links to their appropriate records in the bibliographic file.

Typically, a copy record might include a copy number, a location within the library, a material type designation, the call number, a barcode or optical character number, and perhaps the cost of the copy and the date it was acquired. Usually, creation of copy records coincides with the addition of machine-readable barcode or optical character labels to materials in the library's collections. The MARC format does include a specified format for copy records.

Several options are available for creating copy records in a machine-readable form.

## Option 1

One option for creating machine-readable copy records is to have them generated as pre-processing of bibliographic records prior to loading in local computer storage, described earlier in this chapter, occurs. The following steps describe this option.

1. The library provides copy information for each bibliographic record as it is converted to a machine-readable form. Call numbers, the number of copies owned, and copy locations are provided with the bibliographic records.
2. As a step of pre-processing bibliographic records, the computer generates copy records as specified by the library. A barcode or optical character number can be assigned by the computer to each copy.
3. The computer incorporates the copy records into their corresponding bibliographic records or stores them in a separate file. The link between copy records and their corresponding bibliographic records will be the barcodes or optical character numbers.

The advantages of this option are that the computer can generate copy records and link them to their corresponding bibliographic records as a part of the bibliographic record conversion process, and a means of preparing barcode or optical character number labels can be automatically provided. A disadvantage of this option is that the library staff must incorporate the capture of copy record data into the bibliographic record conversion process.

## Option 2

A second option for creating machine-readable copy records is as a part of the project to barcode a library's collection prior to implementation of an automated circulation function. The following steps describe this option.

1. Shelflist trays and sets of preprinted barcode or optical character labels are taken to the materials in the library's collection.
2. Shelflist cards are matched to the materials.
3. A barcode or optical character label is placed in each copy matched. A duplicate of the label is placed on the shelflist card.
4. Completed trays of cards are taken to a terminal online to the library's computer.
5. The online bibliographic file is searched for matches to the shelflist records with barcode or optical character labels attached.
6. When matching bibliographic records are located, machine-readable copy records are created by manually keying the appropriate information from the shelflist records. If the

terminal has a barcode or optical character scanner, the labels attached to the shelflist cards can be scanned into the file, rather than manually keyed. The copy records are either incorporated into their corresponding bibliographic records or placed in a separate file and linked via the barcode or optical character numbers.

An advantage of this method is that an inventory of the library's collection can be taken as the barcode or optical character number labels are added to materials prior to creation of the copy records. The disadvantages of this option are that the method is time-consuming and highly labor-intensive.

## Option 3

A third option for creating machine-readable copy records is to perform the work at the time materials circulate. The following steps describe this option.

1. A user wishing to borrow specific items from the library's collection brings the materials to the circulation desk.
2. The circulation staff adds a preprinted barcode or optical character label to the copy to be charged out.
3. The staff searches the library's online bibliographic file for the record matching the copy to be circulated.
4. When a matching bibliographic record is located, information for the copy record is manually keyed into the system.
5. The barcode or optical character label on the copy is scanned to add the number to its record.
6. The item is then charged out to the borrower.

An advantage of this option is that not all copy records need be created for the library's collection before an automated circulation function is implemented. A disadvantage of the option is that creating copy records as items circulate makes users wait while the process is completed. This can be particularly irritating to a user with many items to be charged and to other users waiting their turn. Also, some copies of materials may not have bibliographic records on file in the automated function, in which case brief records must be manually keyed into the file before the item can be circulated.

## BORROWER FILES

A file of machine-readable patron or borrower records is required by an automated circulation function. Borrower records usually are brief and well structured. While a MARC record format for borrower records has been proposed, as yet, there is no standard format accepted by the library community. At least two options are available for constructing this file.

## Option 1

Perhaps the most often used method of constructing a borrower file is to create each record manually. The following steps describe this process.

1. A borrower completes a registration form, giving pertinent information such as name, address, telephone number, etc.
2. The borrower gives the registration form to the circulation attendant, who manually keys the information into an online file using a terminal connected to the computer supporting the automated function.
3. The operator assigns a barcode or optical character number to the borrower record. The number is keyed or scanned into the borrower's online record, and the label is attached to a borrower card.
4. The borrower card is given to the user. Some libraries mail the card later to the borrower or have the borrower return at a later time for the card.

An advantage of this option is that no records need be created until users wish to borrow materials. This saves storage space and speeds the response time of the computer as it searches the borrower file. The disadvantage of the option is that staff must manually key each borrower record, causing users charging materials out for the first time to wait for their borrower cards to be prepared, and also causing delays for others at the circulation desk.

## Option 2

A second option for constructing a borrower file is to batch load records from another machine-readable source such as a file of students, faculty, and staff records maintained by the registrar or admissions office of a university or college, the tax rolls of a city or county, or other similar records maintained by the library's parent organization. Special software for extracting the data needed for the library's borrower records and for batch loading the records into a borrower file must be written by or for the library or supplied by the vendor of the automated function.

An advantage of this option is that manual keyboarding of individual borrower records will be eliminated, and the records will be on file and ready to use when borrowers wish to charge out materials. The disadvantage of the option is that records for many people who will never come to the library or wish to check out materials will be added to the borrower file, thus requiring magnetic disk space and possibly reducing response time as the computer searches the file.

## VENDOR FILES

A vendor file containing records for the publishers, jobbers, and other organizations and firms from which the library expects to acquire materials will be required for use with an automated acquisitions function. Vendor records might contain the name, address, and other information such as discounts given and names of sales representatives for each vendor to which the library expects to send purchase orders for materials.

Most likely the only option for creating this file will be to take an existing manual file of vendors to a CRT terminal and manually key the required information into the online file, using software written by or for the library or supplied by the vendor of the automated function. A library may be able to acquire a magnetic tape of vendor information that can be batch loaded into the system, if the software will support this method.

## FUND ACCOUNTING FILES

The library must create a machine-stored fund accounting file for an automated acquisitions function. This file will contain records of each fund account the library wishes to use, the amount of funds allocated to each account, and the names and passwords of those people who will have access to the accounts. The software vendor should assist the library in developing an effective and efficient system of accounts.

## ADDITIONAL READINGS

Adler, Anne G., and Elizabeth A. Baber, eds. *Retrospective Conversion: From Cards to Computer.* Ann Arbor, MI: Pierian Press, 1984.

Boss, Richard W. "Retrospective Conversion: Investing in the Future." *Wilson Library Bulletin* 59 (November 1984): 173-78.

Burger, Robert H. "Conversion of Catalog Records to Machine-Readable Form: Major Projects, Continuing Problems, and Future Prospects." *Cataloging and Classification Quarterly* 3 (Fall 1982): 27-40.

Butler, Brett B., and J.L. Dolby. "Bibliographic Data Bases: Costs and Utility of Conversion." In *Information Roundup, Proceedings of the ASIS 4th Mid-Year Meeting, Portland, Oregon, 15-17 May, 1975.* Washington, DC: ASIS, 1975: 33-43.

Butler, Brett B., Brian Aveney, and William Scholz. "The Conversion of Manual Catalogs to Collection Data Bases." *Library Technology Reports.* 14 (March-April 1978): 109-206.

Carter, Ruth C., and Scott Bruntjen. *Data Conversion.* White Plains, NY: Knowledge Industry Publications, 1983.

Drabenstott, Jon, ed. "Retrospective Conversion: Issues and Perspectives: A Forum." *Library Hi Tech* 4 (Summer 1986): 105-20.

Hudson, Judith. "Bibliographic Record Maintenance in the Online Environment." *Information Technology and Libraries* 3 (December 1984): 388-93.

Johnson, Carolyn A. "Retrospective Conversion of Three Library Collections." *Information Technology and Libraries* 1 (June 1982): 133-39.

Kaplan, Denise P. "Creating Copy Specific Records for Local Databases." *Library Hi Tech* 2 (No.3, 1984): 19-24.

McQueen, Judy, and Richard W. Boss. "Sources of Machine-Readable Cataloging and Retrospective Conversion." *Library Technology Reports* 21 (November-December 1985): 597-732.

Miller, Dan. "Authority Control in the Retrospective Conversion Process." *Library Technology and Libraries* 3 (September 1984): 286-92.

Peters, Stephen H., and Douglas J. Butler. "A Cost Model for Retrospective Conversion Alternatives." *Library Resources & Technical Services* 28 (April/June 1984): 149-51+.

Petersen, K.D. "Planning for Serials Retrospective Conversion." *Serials Review* 10 (Fall 1984): 73-78.

Rice, James. "The Conversion of Library Records to Machine-Readable Form." In *Introduction to Library Automation.* Littleton, CO: Libraries Unlimited, 1984: 147-59.

Sherman, Don. "Converting Bibliographic Records to Machine Form." In *Advances in Librarianship*, edited by Melvin J. Voigt. Vol. 3. New York: Seminar Press, 1972: 221-43.

Valentine, Phyllis A., and David R. McDonald. "Retrospective Conversion: A Question of Time, Standards, and Purpose." *Information Technology and Libraries* 2 (June 1986): 112-20.

# Chapter 10
# Computer Operations

An automated library function will be supported by a computer system located either in the library or elsewhere in a computing center serving the library. The computer may be a microcomputer, a minicomputer, or a mainframe computer, and the staff of the automated function may or may not be responsible directly for supervising its day-to-day operation. However, the librarian must be concerned about the management of the computer system, whether or not the device is under his or her supervision. The librarian must be aware of the basic activities essential to support the automated function. If the computer system is poorly managed, then the operation and success of the automated function will be in jeopardy. Therefore, this chapter includes discussions of:

- Computer operations
- Operations schedules
- Computer site staffing
- Hardware and software maintenance
- Backup systems
- Disaster planning

## COMPUTER OPERATIONS

A computer is an automatic device, in that when it is supplied with a set of instructions and information to be processed, the machine can perform its work without further human intervention. But to support complex library functions, significant human support is needed if the computer is to perform its share of the workload uninterrupted over sustained periods of time. Generally, the larger the computer system, the more complex its support needs will be. The more automated library functions a computer supports, the more difficult it will be to keep the system operating continuously, effectively, and efficiently.

Some of the common tasks people must perform at the computer site in order for a computer system to adequately support an automated library function are briefly described below.

## Starting and Stopping the System

One task humans must perform is to start and stop the computer when necessary. Microcomputers usually are started at the beginning of each work day and stopped at its end. Larger machines usually operate 24 hours a day, day after day, and therefore need be started and stopped only occasionally.

Starting a microcomputer might include inserting a diskette containing the operating system in the disk drive, pushing the "on" switch, and entering the current day and time on the keyboard when prompted. This action loads instructions into the machine's memory that enables it to load other programs. Once the operating system is loaded, the system checks its memory and other components, loads other software as required, and is ready to go to work. For micros with hard disks, the only step might be to push the "on" switch. When the computer is to be stopped, someone must check that all processing has been terminated and all application software has been shut down successfully before turning the machine off and taking any diskettes out of the disk drives for storage until needed again.

Larger computers are started in a manner similar to a microcomputer. Starting a minicomputer or mainframe computer might include turning the machine on and setting some switches on its console. This instructs the machine to load the operating system from a magnetic disk file into memory, load other software as required, check its memory and other devices, and otherwise bring itself to a "ready" state. When the computer is to be stopped, someone must check that all processing has been terminated and all application software has been shut down successfully, just as for the microcomputer, before turning the machine off. Peripheral devices such as printers, communications equipment, and perhaps disk drives may need to be switched on and off separately.

Minicomputers and mainframe computers usually are shut down only while some maintenance operations are being performed. But power, hardware, and software failures will occasionally require that the computer be re-started or re-booted.

## Bringing Application Software Up and Down

A second task humans perform is to bring application software "up" and "down." Starting or booting a computer results in the machine's being brought to a ready state. To use the computer, application software must be loaded and initiated.

Starting or "bringing up" the software that supports an automated acquisitions, circulation, or cataloging function or an online public access catalog requires that the software be loaded into memory, its files and tables opened, and the like. A batch file of commands that will execute these tasks automatically might be used. For example, to start or "bring up" software for an automated acquisitions function, the operator might enter the file name, "ACQUP," into the computer's console keyboard. The computer locates the batch file ACQUP, then executes the commands one after another until the software is "up" and available for use.

Stopping an online is the reverse of starting it. The operator might enter a batch name such as "ACQDOWN" into the console keyboard. The computer locates the batch file, then executes the commands one after another. The commands in the batch file check that no processing activities are in progress, close the files and tables of the function, and make the application software unavailable for use.

Depending upon the sophistication of the hardware, software, and human designers, application software can be brought up and down automatically according to a time schedule. At predetermined times, the computer automatically executes commands in a batch file that will bring the software up. At a preset time, the computer can execute commands in another batch file to bring the software down.

## Monitoring the Computer System

A third task humans must perform is to monitor the computer system supporting the automated function. While staff need neither sit and watch the computer every minute, nor even be in the same room as the computer for extended periods of time, someone does need to check the machine from time to time during the day to make certain that all is going well.

The system should be monitored for disk errors, software errors, printer readiness, and the like. When hardware or software malfunctions occur that affect the operation of the automated function being supported, the staff will report the problem rapidly. Also, the physical environment of the computer system should be monitored for heat build-ups or other factors. A number of electronic sensing devices can be used to monitor the computer system. Sensors can be installed that will detect heat build-up, power fluctuations, power failures, and smoke, and sound a local and/or remote alarm, then activate devices to shut off power or release fire extinguishing agents.

When problems do arise, someone must determine what happened and correct the problem, and restart the hardware and/or software if necessary. Solving problems may be as simple as entering commands or responses on the console keyboard or restarting the software, or as difficult as calling the hardware or software vendor for assistance and having to redo some processing.

## Preparing Backups

A fourth task humans must perform is to prepare copies or "backups" of machine files supporting an automated library function. A backup is a copy of software or files that can be used if the original is destroyed. Reasons why the original might be destroyed include software failures, hardware failures, human errors, fire, water, and even vandalism.

Copies of bibliographic, vendor, borrower, transaction, and other files and the application software are made onto magnetic tape, magnetic disk, or other magnetic media that can store machine-readable files in bulk. For files that change daily as records are added, deleted, or updated, backups should also be made daily. Other files can be backed up less frequently, on a weekly basis or after their records have been updated.

## Initiating and Monitoring Special Batch Programs

A fifth task humans must perform is to initiate and monitor special batch programs. Examples of such programs are for loading and indexing records from magnetic tape, loading and testing new software or enhancements to existing software, extracting records from files in order to prepare special reports, and other housekeeping functions. A person must initiate the batch processes, mount reels of tape, load paper into a printer, respond to error conditions reported by the system, monitor the general progress of the processing, and perform other tasks as required by the process.

## Maintaining Logs of Activities

A sixth task humans must perform is to maintain logs of activities at the computer site. While the computer itself can maintain logs of its internal processing, it cannot keep other records. For example, logs of uptime and downtime for the online systems, records of malfunctions with the hardware and software, times and durations of special batch program runs and problems encountered, and other unusual conditions pertaining to the computer system and the support of the automated function should be maintained. A sample page from a log is shown in Figure 10-1.

The logs will be useful for accountability, training, planning, and scheduling purposes. Also, the hardware and software vendors may

**FIGURE 10-1. Sample Page from the Log of Activities for a Computer System**

| Time | Event |
|------|-------|
| 07:00 a.m. | Brought online system up |
| 07:10 a.m. | Online crashed |
| 07:15 a.m. | Vendor called to explain procedure |
| 07:20 a.m. | Brought online system up again |
| 08:00 a.m. | South Branch reported loss of system |
| 08:05 a.m. | Started record load |
| 08:30 a.m. | Record load finished |
| 08:45 a.m. | Started index build program |
| 09:00 a.m. | Index build stopped |
| 09:15 a.m. | Re-started index build program |
| 10:30 a.m. | Index build finished |
| 12:30 p.m. | Disk drive started making noise |
| 12:35 p.m. | Called vendor for disk maintenance |

require such records to be used in identifying possible causes of hardware and software failures.

## Maintaining the Tape Library

A seventh task humans must perform is to maintain the tape library for the automated library function. For those systems using magnetic tape as a backup medium for software and files, many reels of tape must be handled, stored, retrieved, and recycled. A complete set of backup tapes for all files of an automated function should be stored away from the computer site in case of fire or other calamity at that location. Since the files for any automated function are constantly changing, frequent backups are necessary. New backup copies in the off-site storage locations must be rotated regularly in order to have a recent version of the function's files and software available should recovery be necessary.

## Maintaining an Inventory of Supplies

An eighth task humans must perform is to maintain the inventory of special supplies for the computer system. A computer system requires a variety of special supplies for its effective operation, including blank magnetic tape, diskettes for microcomputers, ribbons for printers, blank fanfold paper, blank custom forms, cleaning supplies for the equipment, etc. Supplies for the automated function itself, such as barcode or OCR labels, bulbs for scanning wands, printer ribbons, blank continuous paper, etc., may also be stored at the in-house computer site for simplicity of supplies management.

A method of reordering supplies when stock is low should be devised. This can be as simple as a checklist of supply amounts from which are subtracted amounts dispensed or used. When the stock reaches a predetermined level, an order for a new supply can be generated. This process can be automated if desired.

## OPERATIONS SCHEDULES

The manager of the automated library function should maintain computer operations schedules that will keep the software supporting the function "up" and available for use as close to 100% of its scheduled uptime as possible. Scheduled uptime for an automated library function may be 16 or more hours a day, five, six, or even seven days a week. During this time, the staff expects to be able to use the automated function without interruption.

A computer system must perform work other than maintaining software up and available, as important as this is. Backups must be prepared, special batch programs must be run, and maintenance must be performed. Most library applications require some special processing, such as data integrity checks, compression of files, deletion of discarded records, rebalancing of files and indexes, compiling required reports, and the like. If the computer is large enough and has sophisticated software, some of this work can be done in the background during the day. That is, the work will be done automatically in between other important tasks the computer performs. But in some cases, computer processing cannot be performed while an automated function is up and being used by staff. If several functions are supported by the same computer system, similar machine tasks are required.

All the work the computer system is to perform must be identified, organized, and scheduled in order to maximize the use of the machine and ensure that the automated function is properly supported. Staff must be available to perform essential tasks at the proper times. Often, the best use of resources can be obtained only after a schedule has been developed, tried, and fine-tuned over a period of weeks or months. As the needs of the automated function for computer support changes, so must the schedule of computer operations.

A sample operations schedule for a computer system supporting a single automated library function is shown in Figure 10-2, and a schedule for a computer system supporting multiple functions in Figure 10-3.

**FIGURE 10-2. A Sample Operations Schedule for a Computer System Supporting a Single Function**

| Time | Event |
|------|-------|
| 06:45 a.m. | Check previous night's processing |
| 07:00 a.m. | Bring online up |
| 07:30 a.m. | Start overdues compile |
| 08:00 a.m. | Print overdues |
| 10:00 p.m. | Bring online down |
| 10:05 p.m. | Backup all files |
| 11:00 p.m. | Start overnight processing batch |

**FIGURE 10-3. A Sample Operations Schedule for a Computer System Supporting Multiple Functions**

| Time | Event |
|------|-------|
| 06:30 a.m. | Check system for problems, overnight processing, etc. |
| 06:35 a.m. | Bring circulation online up |
| 06:40 a.m. | Bring acquisitions online up |
| 06:45 a.m. | Bring cataloging online up |
| 06:50 a.m. | Bring online catalog up |
| 07:30 a.m. | Start circulation overdues compile |
| 08:00 a.m. | Print overdues |
| 09:00 a.m. | Print yesterday's purchase orders |
| 10:00 a.m. | Print and distribute reports |
| 10:00 p.m. | Bring acquisitions online down |
| 10:05 p.m. | Backup acquisitions files |
| 10:30 p.m. | Start acquisitions overnight processing batch |
| 10:35 p.m. | Bring cataloging online down |
| 10:40 p.m. | Backup cataloging files |
| 11:15 p.m. | Start cataloging overnight processing batch |
| 11:20 p.m. | Bring circulation online down |
| 11:25 p.m. | Backup circulation files |
| 12:00 p.m. | Start circulation overnight processing batch |
| 12:05 p.m. | Bring online catalog down |
| 12:10 p.m. | Run online catalog statistics |
| 12:15 p.m. | Bring online catalog back up for dial-in users |

## COMPUTER OPERATIONS STAFFING

The manager of the automated library function should be concerned that adequate staffing is provided to perform the support tasks required by the computer system. The amount of staff time needed will depend upon the type of automated function being supported by the computer system, the size of the computer, the number of applications the computer is supporting, the size of the application databases, the amount of time the library is open, and the automated functions being used.

If a microcomputer supports an automated function, then one person can easily handle all the required work on a part-time basis, devoting perhaps an average of an hour a day to computer operations.

A medium-sized library with minicomputer-based functions may require as many as two or more full-time equivalent staff to do nothing but maintain the computer system. Larger systems will require even more staff.

Supervising the computer site may not be the responsibility of the manager of the automated library function. The management of an in-house computer system might be under the supervision of an automation or systems librarian serving the entire library. If the computer system is not in the library but elsewhere in a computing center serving the library, its operations staff may be supervised by someone at that location. In the latter case, computer operations and schedules must be closely coordinated with library staff.

## HARDWARE AND SOFTWARE MAINTENANCE

Any computer system supporting an automated library function will require maintenance periodically throughout its lifetime. Both hardware and software maintenance will be necessary. The significance of this to the librarian is that, while maintenance is being performed, the computer system might not be available to support the automated function.

### Hardware Maintenance

The hardware of a computer system will require maintenance from time to time. Two types of maintenance usually are necessary.

The first type of hardware maintenance is referred to as corrective maintenance. Corrective or remedial maintenance is needed on an on-call, unscheduled basis to correct equipment malfunctions. Corrective maintenance can be obtained through a contract with a vendor, or on a per-problem basis. A hardware maintenance contract will cost approximately 10% of the original purchase price of a piece of equipment per year. For example, a maintenance contract for a device costing $3,000 to purchase will cost $300 per year. The contract will cover parts and labor required during the period of the contract to repair the piece of equipment. Without a maintenance contract, the library must pay separately for correcting each problem that arises. While a maintenance contract may not be recommended for a microcomputer system, one usually is essential for larger machines, due to their complexity.

The offending device may be repaired on-site, picked up by the maintenance staff and taken to a repair shop, or the library staff may take or mail the device to the repair shop. Some spare parts may be retained at the computer system and used to repair defective parts as needed.

The second type of hardware maintenance is referred to as preventive maintenance. Preventive maintenance includes tests, replacements, adjustments, and necessary repairs carried out on a scheduled basis and intended to prevent future malfunctions from occurring. This maintenance is designed to keep hardware in good operating condition and therefore minimize corrective maintenance. It may be performed by the same vendor who supplies corrective maintenance, under the same contract.

## Software Maintenance

Software maintenance also will be necessary. It usually is acquired through a warranty or contract arrangement with the designer or vendor of the software. A software maintenance contract will cost about 10% of the original purchase cost of the software per year.

Software maintenance can be provided in several ways. One method is for software maintenance staff to dial into the computer system and correct malfunctions or problems with the software from a distance. This method usually is fast, once the maintenance staff begins work. A second method is for the software designer or vendor to mail fixes for problems and malfunctions of the software on diskettes or magnetic tape to the computer site. Staff then must load the corrections, following instructions provided.

## BACKUP SYSTEMS

There is no known automated library function that will be available for use 100% of the time it is needed. Some factors that might cause an automated function to be unavailable for a period of time include:

1. Hardware failures
2. Software failures
3. Communication line failures
4. Loss of air conditioning in the computer room, thus causing shutdown of the computer system
5. Loss of electricity
6. Human errors

An automated function may be available 99% of the time during a day, week, or month, but staff and users must be able to continue their work or use of the library and its services during that remaining 1%. A library may have an automated function available 100% of the time three months in a row, but only 90% of the time in the fourth month. Backups for various automated library functions are discussed below.

## Backup for an Automated Acquisitions Function

An automated acquisitions function usually does not have a backup in case hardware or software are unable to support it. Since the public is not directly and immediately affected should an acquisitions function not be available, most libraries feel that a delay of an hour or a day will not seriously affect its services. However, staff of the acquisitions function may be left with no work to perform until the system is once again available. This is particularly true after a library eliminates its manual files and depends totally upon the online system. In this case, each staff member should be trained to perform work in other areas of the library. If the automated procedures are to be unavailable for long periods of time, the staff should move to their "backup" jobs.

## Backup for an Automated Cataloging Function

As for an automated acquisitions function, no backup system usually is provided for automated cataloging. Staff also can move to secondary jobs or tasks until the automated procedures are once again available.

## Backup for an Online Public Access Catalog

Until the online public access catalog is fully developed, tested, and stable, the card catalog can be retained as its backup. When the online catalog is down, users can be directed to the card catalog to locate materials in the library's collection. But once the online catalog is reliable, most libraries close or discard their card catalogs. In this case, several types of backups have been used. For the very small online catalog, printouts of the files can be used until the system is again available. For larger systems, backup catalogs on microfilm, microfiche, or optical disk can be provided. These backups can be prepared in various ways from the database supporting the online catalog.

## DISASTER PLANNING

The manager of the automated library function should insist that a good disaster plan is in place for the computer system. Disasters to the computer that might affect the automated function include disk head crashes, fire, severe storms and flooding, and malicious damage and vandalism.

A plan to be followed in case of a disaster will enable the library to recover its computing power and thus its automated functions in the shortest possible time. The plan may never have to be used, but if disaster does strike, the library could recover and be back in operation rapidly.

Keeping backups of all software and files in a location away from the computer site is a start. If calamity hits the computer site, the backups can be used to restore the system to the computer supporting the automated function or to another computer. It is expensive and time-consuming to prepare and maintain backups of files on a regular basis, but it is sound management practice to do so.

A sample disaster procedure for a fire emergency is shown in Figure 10-4.

### FIGURE 10-4. A Sample Disaster Procedure for a Fire Emergency at a Computer Site

If fire is discovered at the computer site, do not endanger yourself. Take the following action:

1. Press the red emergency-off button on the power control unit.

2. Set off the alarm located beside the office of the acquisitions librarian.

3. If the library is open, begin informing staff and users to evacuate the building.

4. If the fire seems small enough to be easily and immediately contained, use the fire extinguisher in the computer room until the fire department arrives.

5. If there seems to be no chance of controlling the fire or containing it to a particular area, leave the room and close the computer room door.

6. Notify the manager-on-call.

Recovery from a fire in the computer room will depend upon the severity of the damage. Take the following action:

1. Call the vendor to come and assess the damage to the computer equipment.

   a. If the damage is not severe, have the vendor repair or replace any necessary parts.

   b. If the damage is severe, have the vendor assess the damage and present a report to the library administration.

2. When the systems have been thoroughly checked out, determine if the data files and software are intact. Restore software and files as necessary.

3. Re-boot the systems and conduct tests to ensure that they are in good working condition.

4. Bring up the online systems.

## ADDITIONAL READINGS

Brooks, Bill. "Computer Operations Management." In *Handbook of Computer Management*, by R.B. Yearsley and G.M.R. Graham. New York: Halsted Press, 1973: 151-67.

Condon, Robert J. "Managing the Systems and Data Processing Areas." In *Data Processing Systems Analysis and Design*. 2nd ed. Reston, VA: Reston Publishing Company, 1978: 291-307.

McFarlan, F. Warren, and Richard L. Nolan, eds. *The Information Systems Handbook*. New York: Dow Jones-Irwin, 1975.

Schaeffer, Howard. *Data Center Operations: A Guide to Effective Planning, Processing, and Performance*. 2nd ed. New York: Prentice-Hall, 1987.

Svobodova, Liba. *Computer Performance Measurement and Evaluation Methods: Analysis and Applications*. New York: American Elsevier Publishing, 1976.

Wadsworth, M.D. *The Human Side of Data Processing Management*. New York: Prentice-Hall, 1973.

# Chapter 11
# Automated Function
# Activation and Evaluation

Once a function has been reorganized, space and workstations have been renovated or constructed, documentation has been prepared, the staff have been trained, and all essential files have been created, the automated routines can be activated. This process often is referred to as "bringing up the system" or "going live with the system." Then, after the automated function has been activated, it must be evaluated and corrective action taken should the function not be operating as anticipated. This chapter includes discussions of:

- Activation options
- Evaluation of the automated function
- Fine-tuning the automated function

## ACTIVATION OPTIONS

There are several approaches to activating an automated library function, each with its own particular advantages and disadvantages for a specific project. How an automated function is activated will depend upon the nature of the function, its size, and its users. For example, an approach to activating an automated circulation function should minimize service disruptions to users. An automated acquisitions function, on the other hand, may be activated in a more leisurely manner. Any option chosen for activating an automated function should, however, be well-planned and well-managed.

### Total Approach

One option for activating an automated function is the *total* or *all-at-once approach.* In this case, old procedures are abandoned completely on a given date and time, and the automated routines take their place. This approach is by far the most demanding of all methods, and requires that:

1. All phases of the activation be carefully planned and coordinated.
2. Hardware and software be thoroughly tested and checked.
3. The essential machine-readable files be created, loaded, and tested.
4. Staff be well oriented and trained in advance to operate and manage the new function.

## Pilot Approach

Another option for activating an automated function is called the *pilot approach*. In this case, the automated procedures are activated first in only one department or branch of the library, then later in others when it is certain that the new routines are working properly. For example, an automated circulation function can be activated first in a small branch library, then later in the main library where will be found a higher volume of activities and problems. This method is effective when the library has several relatively self-contained and geographically separate branches or departments.

The advantages of the pilot approach to activating an automated function are that:

1. It permits the selection of the particular organizational unit in which the staff are most ready to accept the automated function, while installation in other units need not begin until everyone is satisfied that the pilot installation is running smoothly.
2. The most critical problems with the automated procedures can be detected and resolved in a low-volume environment.
3. The successful operation of the automated procedures in one department or branch can strongly motivate hesitant staff in other units.
4. The activation of the automated function on a small scale can usually be accomplished more quickly than activation by the all-at-once approach and permits the overall installation to progress at a more relaxed pace.

## Phased Approach

A third option for activating an automated function is called the *phased approach*. In this case, the automated function is separated into a number of modules or subfunctions that are activated, tested, evaluated, and fine-tuned one at a time. For example, the order preparation activities of an automated acquisitions function may be activated first, then the order preparation activities, then the receiving activities, then finally the fund accounting activities.

Although this option takes longer than others, there is more time to work with the problems that arise in the individual parts. Unfortunately, not every automated function can be installed in this manner because it may not be possible to separate it into significant, relatively independent parts.

## Parallel Approach

A fourth option for activating an automated function is called the *parallel method*. In this case, the old and the new routines are operated side by side for a period of time. The old system is gradually or suddenly phased out as soon as the automated function is performing satisfactorily. For example, the card catalog can be retained and kept current after an online public access catalog is activated until the latter has been thoroughly evaluated and fine-tuned. Another example might be parallel serials check-in functions. The manual method of checking-in serial issues can operate side-by-side with automated check-in of the same issues for a period of time.

The parallel approach is best when the consequences of failing to produce satisfactory results with the automated function would be disastrous. It is the most conservative and costliest of the approaches, because two systems must be operated simultaneously to perform the same functions. This requires additional staff time and can result in delays in service or reduced output. On the other hand, this approach does permit staff to solve problems encountered with the new procedures before abandoning the old ones.

## EVALUATION OF THE AUTOMATED FUNCTION

After an automated library function has been activated, it should be evaluated to determine if it is performing as expected or as required to meet contractual agreements with the vendor of the hardware and/or software. Several common evaluations of the automated function can be made.

### Evaluating the Automated Function's Reliability

One common evaluation of an automated function is its reliability. Reliability here is defined as the ability of the automated function to operate at a specified level of effectiveness for a stated period of time.

*Example*: The automated function is expected to operate reliably for a period of 45 (or 60 or 90) consecutive days at an uptime level of 95% (or 96% or 97%).

The meaning of "uptime" must be agreed upon by the library and the vendor before the test is begun.

*Example*: Uptime shall mean the operational use time (the amount of time the function should be available for use by the library) minus downtime (the amount of time the function is not available for use by the library due to hardware or software malfunctions) divided by the operational use time:

Uptime = (Operational Use Time) minus (Downtime)/Operational Use Time

Thus, the uptime for a function with an operational use time of 24 hours a day, but which was down two hours, will be:

Uptime = (24-2)/24 or 91.7%

A common problem that the library might encounter is that a part of an automated function will be down for a period of time, but other parts will be operating satisfactorily. For example, a light pen will cease functioning, but the remainder of the function is performing well. While this will be of a noncritical nature, other function parts, such as a disk drive or the software that permits check-outs in an automated circulation function, are critical and would seriously affect use of the system. For these reasons, some libraries define a level of reliability based upon downtime of various components of the function.

*Example*: The downtime factor shall be calculated by multiplying the downtime hours (those daily operational hours between the time the vendor has been notified of a function failure and the time the function is fully operating again) by a downtime coefficient. Total function downtime shall equal the sum of the downtime factors divided by the sum of daily library operation hours.

The coefficients then must be defined for both critical and noncritical operations failures.

*Example*: The coefficients for critical operations failures shall be defined as follows:

Catalog Record Creation  . . . . . . . . . . . . . . .  1.0
Online Catalog Searches . . . . . . . . . . . . . . .  1.0
Charge and Discharge  . . . . . . . . . . . . . . . .  1.0
Holds and Renewals  . . . . . . . . . . . . . . . . .  1.0
Borrower Record Creation  . . . . . . . . . . . . .  1.0
Requisition Order Preparation . . . . . . . . . . .  1.0
Receiving Materials . . . . . . . . . . . . . . . . . .  1.0

*Example*: The coefficients for noncritical operations failures, such as report printing, shall be 0.25 after a 24-hour grace period.

*Example*: Other software failures not significantly affecting operation of the function shall have a coefficient of 0.1 beginning five days after a call to the vendor for service.

Coefficients for hardware failures should also be defined. For example:

```
Central Processing Unit . . . . . . . . . . . . . . . .   1.0
Disk Drive . . . . . . . . . . . . . . . . . . . . . . . .   1.0
Tape Drive . . . . . . . . . . . . . . . . . . . . . . . .   1.0
Line Printer  . . . . . . . . . . . . . . . . . . . . . .   1.0
CRT Terminal . . . . . . . . . . . . .  0.1 Per Terminal
Optical Scanner . . . . . . . . . . . .  0.1 Per Scanner
Communications Equipment  . . . . . .  0.1 Per Piece
```

Thus, if during a 45-day reliability test period (or 450 hours at ten hours operational use time daily) the charge activity was down for four hours, a disk drive for two hours, and a terminal for 20 hours, the calculations for downtime would be as follows:

```
Charge Activity . . . . . . . . . . . .   1.0 x 4 Hours = 4
Disk Drive  . . . . . . . . . . . . . .   1.0 x 2 Hours = 2
Terminal . . . . . . . . . . . . . . . .   0.1 x 20 Hours = 2
Total  . . . . . . . . . . . . . . . . . . . . . . . . . . . . .   8
```

The downtime for the 45-day period will be 8/450 or 1.7%. Conversely, the uptime will be 98.3%, or the downtime subtracted from 100%.

The library should notify the vendor of the automated function when the reliability test period will begin. If desired, the vendor can be reminded of the terms of the test. Logs of downtime should be maintained by the library during the test, with times recorded to the nearest one-tenth of an hour when a component of the function becomes inoperable and again when the item is made operational.

The library should state in writing what will happen should the function not pass the reliability test.

*Example*: In the event of a failure on the part of the automated function to meet the 95% (or 96% or 97%) uptime minimum, the 45 (or 60 or 90) consecutive day reliability test shall begin anew.

A part of the library's payment to the vendor can be predicated upon the passing of the reliability test by the automated function.

## Evaluating the Function's Performance

Another means of evaluating the automated function is on its performance, that is, on whether or not the function performs as was advertised or contracted for by the library. For example, in an automated cataloging function, the vendor might have promised that the software would allow the correction of all fields of a bibliographic record before it is updated by the computer. The staff discover that the system requires that each line be updated separately. Or the vendor promised that entries in an index would be automatically updated when changes in a bibliographic record are made, but the system actually requires an overnight batch update of the index.

If an automated function is carefully tested and checked before it is activated, most problems with its performance will be detected and corrected beforehand. But often, even after careful testing, some problems will not be noticed until after the automated function has been activated and is in a "live" mode. The reason might be that particular conditions were not tested or situations did not occur in the test that would have detected a problem. This is normal and should not be of great concern to the librarian.

## Evaluating the Computer System's Response Time

Another means of evaluating the automated function is the response time of its supporting computer. A response time test can be conducted to determine if the function can perform operations and tasks with an acceptable response time at the rates or levels specified by the library and advertised by the vendor.

*Example*: A full-load response time test shall be conducted on-site after the vendor has installed the system and has certified in writing that the function is operational and after all software has been installed and accepted by the library.

*Example*: The response time test shall provide unequivocal evidence (i.e., the results may be entered into a written log) that the system meets response time performance requirements under a peak load condition.

In short, this test measures the time required for the computer system to complete typical transactions. The time required for the system to complete a transaction must be carefully defined.

*Example*: Response time means the elapsed time between the submission or command (the pressing of the "enter" or "send" key) and the return of the complete response to the operator (the screen is filled).

*Example*: Response time means the time between the pressing of the enter or send key after entry of queries or commands and the time the first character of the system's response is displayed on the screen.

The load on the system during the test should be specified by the library.

*Example*: A library-specified mix of terminal dedications; e.g., 50% of the terminals dedicated to charging items, 10% to discharging items, and 40% to data inputs/edits, with the printing of overdue notices in a background job.

*Example*: A library-specified "peak load" or "worst case" job mix; e.g., 1,000 charge and renewal transactions, 200 discharges, 200 file inquiries (100 of which are bibliographic inquiries), 100 data input/edits, and two batch jobs, in a single hour.

In addition, the acceptable response times for various activities should be specified by the library.

*Example*: The system shall, operating in the worst case test, exhibit response times not exceeding:
   Six seconds for data input/edit
   Four seconds for file inquiries
   Two seconds for charge, renewal, discharge, and other circulation
      tasks.

The response time test should be carefully planned in advance. The library's automation librarian can assist in designing and setting up the test. The library should provide operators, test log keepers, and data recorders for each terminal during the test. Stop watches may be used to measure response times. Vendor representatives should be present during the test, if possible. Should the system not pass the response time test, additional tests can be conducted after the vendor has had time to make adjustments to the software or hardware. The library may withhold payment or partial payment until the response time test has been passed.

## FINE-TUNING THE AUTOMATED FUNCTION

After evaluations of the automated library function have been completed and problems have been detected, corrections should be made. Also, the manager should be alert to bottlenecks in workflow or other situations that need fine-tuning. For example, it might have been thought during the planning stages of an automated circulation function that three overdue notices would be necessary and desirable. But, after the function has been operating for a month or two, the manager discovers that two notices will actually be sufficient. The software then can be altered to produce only two notices rather than three.

Fine-tuning an automated function might go on for a year after activation. Often, experimentation with procedures, the duties and responsibilities of staff, the location of workstations, and other aspects of the automated function is highly desirable to determine best means of maximizing the benefits of automation. This requires trial and error on the manager's part, or at least a trial, evaluation of the results, then, if necessary, altering the situation in the manner indicated.

## ADDITIONAL READINGS

"Automating Libraries: The Major Mistakes Vendors Are Likely to Make." *Library Hi Tech* 3 (No. 2, 1985): 107-13.

Corbin, John. "System Activation." In *Managing the Library Automation Project*. Phoenix: Oryx Press, 1985: 178-80.

Epstein, Susan B. "Testing and More Testing." *Library Journal* 110 (July 1985): 40-41.

————. "Testing: Did You Get What You Bought?" *Library Journal* 110 (May 1, 1985): 34-35.

Hayes, Robert M., and Joseph Becker. "System Implementation." In *Handbook of Data Processing for Libraries*. 2nd ed. Los Angeles: Melville Publishing, 1974: 195-213.

Matthews, Joseph R. "Benchmark and Acceptance Tests: Why and When to Use Them." *Library Hi Tech* 4 (Fall 1986): 43-50.

Norton, N.P.A. "A Quality Assurance Program for an Online Library System." In *Conference on Integrated Online Library Systems (2nd: 1984: Atlanta, GA). Second National Conference on Integrated Online Library Systems*. Canfield, OH: Genaway & Associates, 1984: 277-85.

Rice, James. "Installing, Using, and Evaluating the New System." In *Introduction to Library Automation*. Littleton, CO: Libraries Unlimited, 1984: 160-69.

Sugnet, Chris, ed. "System Performance: A Forum." *Library Hi Tech* 4 (Fall 1986): 93-103.

# Index

### by Debbie Burnham-Kidwell

JOHN CORBIN is Associate Professor, School of Library and Information Sciences, University of North Texas, Denton, TX. His previous positions have included Assistant Director for Automation and Systems, University of Houston; Associate Director for Technical Services, Stephen F. Austin State University, Nacogdoches, TX; Planning Officer, Colorado State Library, Denver, CO; Director of Automation Services, Tarrant County Junior College, Ft. Worth, TX; Director of Technical Services, Texas State Library, Austin, TX; and Acquisitions Librarian, University of Texas at Arlington. He holds a Ph.D. in Library Systems Management from the University of Oklahoma and an M.L.S. from the University of Texas at Austin. He has published numerous articles on various aspects of library automation, technical services, and networking. His published books include *Managing the Library Automation Project* (Oryx Press, 1985); *Developing Computer-Based Library Systems* (Oryx Press, 1981); *Computer-Based Acquisitions Procedures at Tarrant County Junior College District* (LARC Press, 1974); *A Technical Services Manual for Small Libraries* (Scarecrow Press, 1971); and *Index of State Geological Survey Publications Issued in Series* (Scarecrow Press, 1965). In 1981, he was named Texas Librarian of the Year by the Texas Library Association, and in 1970 he received the Esther J. Piercy Award from the Resources and Technical Services Division of the American Library Association.